Speaking Out
Jewish Voices
from United Germany

Speaking Out
Jewish Voices
from United Germany

Susan Stern
Editor

Photographs by Todd Weinstein

edition q
Chicago, Berlin, Tokyo, and Moscow

edition q, inc.
551 North Kimberly Drive
Carol Stream, IL 60188

Library of Congress Cataloging-In-Publication Data

Speaking out: Jewish voices from united Germany/Susan Stern, editor.
    p.   cm.
ISBN 1–883695–08–2
1. Jews—Germany—History—1945. 2. Holocaust survivors—Germany—Biography. 3. Germany—Ethnic relations. I. Stern, Susan.
DS135.G332S68 1995
943'.004924-dc20   95–15752
                                                                          CIP

Die Deutsche Bibliothek—CIP-Einheitsaufnahme
Speaking out: Jewish voices from united germany/Susan Stern (ed.).—Berlin, Chicago; Tokyo; Moscow: Ed. q, 1995; ISBN 1–883695–08–2
NE: Stern, Susan (Hrsg.)

Published with the support of Atlantik-Brücke

Printed in Germany

Contents

Acknowledgements

Speaking Out: Jewish Voices from United Germany was realized under the auspices of Atlantik-Brücke (Atlantic Bridge), a private, non-partisan and non-profit organization founded in 1952 and dedicated to improving relations between Germans and North Americans. As an important part of its function, Atlantik-Brücke works closely with Jewish organizations in the United States (the American Jewish Committee and the Armonk Institute) to promote understanding between Germans and American Jews. Contacts between the German and American organizations are frequent; one of the most intensive is a several-day meeting which takes place every year in the United States, Germany or Israel between a delegation of Germans invited by Atlantik-Brücke and representatives and guests of the American Jewish Committee. Among its other activities in this area, Atlantik-Brücke has set up a Standing Committee for German/American-Jewish Questions; the committee meets in Bonn twice a year.

The publication of *Speaking Out* has been made possible through the generous donations to Atlantik-Brücke by the following companies and foundations:

Allianz Versicherungs AG
Bayerische Motoren-Werke (BMW) AG
Degussa-Konrad-Henkel-Stiftung
Deutsche Bank AG

Deutsche Vermögensberatung AG
Hoechst AG
Landeszentralbank in Nordrhein-Westfalen
Preussag AG
Rütgerswerke AG
VEBA AG

The editor of *Speaking Out* would like to convey her personal thanks to all those who contributed financially to the project, as well as to Professor Dieter Feddersen for his legal advice.

Credits

All of the chapters with the exception of the introduction and the articles by Igor Reichlin and Sofia Mill were translated from the German by Doris Jones, with support from Paul Keast and Jeremy Gaines. Sofia Mill's chapter was translated from the Russian by Igor Reichlin.

A special word of thanks to Doris Jones, who did far more than just translate and provided invaluable help in editing the material.

The contribution of Elvira Grözinger, who in addition to writing a chapter was very generous with her contacts and influence, is much appreciated.

★★★

The publisher wishes to express gratitude for permission to translate into English and print the following two selections:

Michael Wolffsohn: "Um einen Nationalismus von innen bittend" from *Verwirrtes Deutschland?* edition ferenczy bei Bruckmann, Munich 1993

Richard Chaim Schneider: excerpts from *Zwischenwelten*, Kindler Verlag, Munich 1994

Preface

When *Speaking Out: Jewish Voices from United Germany* was still no more than an idea being discussed by Atlantik-Brücke and editor Susan Stern, it was not planned as a book to mark a particular occasion. And yet, the fact that it is appearing in 1995 is most certainly significant. For 1995 is a special year; a year of remembrance and commemoration, the 50th anniversary of the end of the Second World War. It was in the spring of 1945 that Germany capitulated; it was during 1945 that the concentration and death camps were liberated. The victims of these inhuman institutions were not all Jewish, but vast numbers were—90 percent in the case of Auschwitz, where around 1.5 million Jews were killed. And thus it is inevitable that 1995 should become a year in which the long and complex relationship between Jews and Germans is reviewed and reassessed with particular feeling and intensity. The horrors of the Holocaust are chillingly revived, in part to ensure that history will never repeat itself.

While the past is the focus of the anniversary ceremonies, the occasion is an altogether appropriate one to ponder the present and the future. For the closing of a chapter in history simultaneously marks the opening of the next, and following the end of hostilities 50 years ago, a new and constructive era began. It could not change or undo the past, but much has been accomplished in the intervening decades. In 1945, the Jewish community that had existed before the war was decimated, exterminated; to many, it was inconceivable that there could ever be another Jewish community on German soil. But the fact is that in 1995, there is. It is a fraction of the size of the prewar community, the majority of its members are no longer Jews of German ancestry, but 50 years later, it is a solid, thriving community with its own institutions, a diverse cultural life, a growing self-confidence and a voice that is heard frequently on a wide range of topics throughout the country and beyond.

It would be naive to imagine that only half a century after the Holocaust the Jewish community in Germany could be free of the trauma; that worry and fear could have ceased to exist; that relations between Jews and Germans could be called "normal." There are still survivors with first-hand memories, and the succeeding generations have not escaped without deep, perhaps permanent scars. Jewish life in Germany today is not, indeed could not be, unencumbered. But it is nevertheless a new life, flourishing in its complexes and complexity.

As part of its effort to promote better understanding about the new Jewish population in Germany, Atlantik-Brücke is happy to be able to offer this English-language book containing essays by some of the most prominent and outspoken Jews living in Germany. Susan Stern has not shied away from controversial opinion; through her choice of contributions, she has tried to convey some of the many facets of the Jewish soul and the Jewish situation. Given the sensitivity of the topic and the taboos surrounding it, the task was not an easy one; she was often called meshugge by fellow Jews and non-Jews alike who doubted that she could produce a balanced picture. We at Atlantik-Brücke think she has, and we are very grateful to her. We believe that *Speaking Out: Jewish Voices from United Germany* is a valuable contribution to the ongoing discussion on Jews in Germany.

Walther Leisler Kiep   Beate Lindemann
Chairman   Executive Vice Chairman

                 Atlantik-Brücke e.V.
                 Bonn and Berlin

11

Explanation of Terms

The following terms recur frequently in the chapters of this book. Wherever they appear, they have been marked with an asterisk.

Allgemeine Jüdische Wochenzeitung: Official newspaper of the Central Council of Jews in Germany.

Bitburg: Location of a military cemetery where Chancellor Helmut Kohl invited President Ronald Reagan to pay joint homage to the war dead in May 1985, in the spirit of reconciliation and normalcy. Since there are graves of SS soldiers at the Bitburg cemetery, the ceremony caused widespread outrage, especially among the Jewish population. Appeals to have the visit canceled were, however, to no avail.

Der Spiegel: A left-of-center weekly magazine known for its thorough investigative journalism and in-depth articles.

Fassbinder Dispute: An uproar caused by the intention to stage Rainer Werner Fassbinder's play *Garbage, the City and Death* in Frankfurt in 1985. The premiere was physically blocked by protesting citizens, most of them from the Jewish community, who found the play, and particularly the character of the Rich Jew, outrageously anti-Semitic. Not only the premiere, but the entire production was canceled.

Frankfurter Allgemeine Zeitung: Germany's leading right-of-center national newspaper.

Historians' Debate (*Historikerstreit*): The attempt by some historians including Ernst Nolte★ to relativize the Holocaust and thereby deny its uniqueness caused a lively, often acrimonious debate among historians and philosophers.

Kristallnacht (The Night of Broken Glass): The night of November 9, 1938, when Nazi mobs went on a well-organized nationwide rampage against the Jews and their property. Many Jews were beaten and killed, or rounded up and sent to concentration camps; synagogues were fire-bombed, homes were destroyed. The name *Kristallnacht* came from the shattering of window glass.

Nolte, Ernst: One of Germany's most controversial right-wing historians who argues that the Holocaust was not unique, but can be compared to the atrocities committed in the Soviet Union under Stalin. The publication in 1986 of Nolte's article entitled "Das Vergehen der Vergangenheit" (The Fading Away of the Past) in the *Frankfurter Allgemeine Zeitung*★ became part of what is known as the Historians' Debate★.

Nuremberg Laws: The laws enacted in 1935 which excluded Jews from German citizenship and prohibited marriage and intimate relations between Jews and non-Jews.

Reichskristallnacht: See **Kristallnacht**.

Shoah: The Hebrew word for catastrophe which has become synonymous with the Holocaust.

Introduction

by Susan Stern

The idea to put together a book of essays by Jews living in Germany came to me in early 1993. I was in New York, the guest of Atlantik-Brücke and the American Jewish Committee at a conference on current concerns in Germany and in German/American-Jewish relations. At the end of the conference, I was invited to a large Upper West Side synagogue together with Ignatz Bubis, head of the Jewish Community in Germany, and the German journalist Thomas Kielinger. In a podium discussion called "Germany—can the nightmare recur?" we were asked to share our views on neo-Nazism and other potential threats to German democracy. Of course, we all three deplored the recent horrifying incidents of right-wing extremist violence against foreigners (this was shortly after the arson deaths in Mölln) and the increase in overt xenophobia, but we still saw no signs of a popular (a mass or well organized) neo-Nazi movement or of any serious threat to Germany's firmly anchored democratic structures. The audience listened to us politely, they asked intelligent and informed questions. At the end of the evening, however, it was quite clear that our non-hysterical approach to the situation in Germany, our confidence that the nightmare would and could not recur (at least, not in Germany in the foreseeable future) in no way coincided with the prevailing opinion in the auditorium. What we had to say made very little impression—we were written off as gullible and naive. No matter that we lived in Germany and could presumably judge the climate better than from afar. No matter that Ignatz Bubis, the official voice of 43,000 Jews in Germany, was himself a survivor. For most people in attendance that evening, Germany remained a country of ex- and potential murderers, and another Holocaust was a real and present danger.

And inevitably, the question of questions was asked by almost everyone who came up to us during the post-discussion reception: how can you, a Jew, live in Germany? I don't remember what answers I gave, since I have so many of them to be delivered as appropriate. I do remember that I felt particularly frustrated at the unwillingness of this educated American public to see modern Germany as anything other than the Germany of the 1930s.

Later that same year, I spoke to several different Jewish organizations during a coast-to-coast lecture tour. My topic: Jews in Germany, who they are, how they see themselves and how others see them. The older audiences in particular—the survivor generation—seemed happy to have some of their fears about the situation in Germany allayed, and on several occasions I was thanked emotionally for bringing a good-news message. I'm not so sure that I got through to some of the younger public, who seemed to regard me as a government emissary, paid to spread pro-German propaganda.

At any rate, I had already decided to put together a book, to ask some fellow Jewish residents of the Federal Republic to describe various aspects of Jewish life here—first and foremost to show that there really is Jewish life here—and to articulate their feelings about living in a country which in the eyes of many outsiders, no self-respecting Jew should ever set foot in. Clearly, the essays would reflect a complex reality. The very fact that Jews in Germany are willy-nilly on the defensive, that they are required by a critical, at times hostile Jewish world to justify their existence in the country they have chosen as their home, is an enormous psychological burden. Far greater in many cases is the burden of having to justify the choice to themselves. But one way or another, the choice has been made by well over 50,000 Jews, and this in itself, I believe, is testimony to the viability of Jewish life in modern Germany.

In any event, the decision to settle or remain in Germany is a theme that several of the authors talk about very personally in their contributions to *Speaking Out*. For Ralph Giordano, a survivor, the question is central. "Why I have remained" is his subtitle, and to come up with his reasons, he has to dig into a painful past. He comes to the conclusion that, in part, it is precisely because of the past, the Holocaust, his relationship to the victims, the lesson to be learned from Auschwitz ("Never again") that he had to stay. Moreover, it has become clear to him—"one of the most valuable realizations of my life"—that the vast majority of Germans, and not just isolated individuals, are comrades, "the humus of my new feeling of belonging." Ralph Giordano, one of Germany's most watchful and at times fiercest critics, is, in his own words, "nailed to the country." And after much consideration, to the question "Is Germany becoming dangerous again?" his answer is a qualified but unmistakeable no.

The same answer, less hedged, is given by Ernst Cramer, also a survivor who is haunted—in his article, almost lyrically—by his memories. As he surveys the current scene of radical violence on both extremes of the political spectrum, he talks in terms of déjà vu. But he is very convinced that what is happening now is not a prelude to a repeat of the 1930s and 1940s; democracy in Germany today, says Cramer, is so firmly anchored that it cannot be endangered by fringe groups. "I view the future with confidence."

A member of a different generation, the historian Julius Schoeps, born in Sweden in 1942, talks about the double bind that confronts many Jews who have opted for a life in Germany. On the one hand, they are forced into the defensive by their fellow Jews outside Germany who have no understanding for their choice of homeland, and who show little tolerance. On the other hand, since their choice has been voluntary, since they have in some way made their peace with Germany, they have their own diffuse feelings of guilt to live with, and these may weigh heavily. It is paradoxical, concludes Schoeps, that for some, this inner torment has even become a kind of justification for staying.

Richard Schneider, over a decade younger than Julius Schoeps (as he puts it himself, one of the generation now going on 40) was born in Germany. But this has not made life easier for him; of all the authors in *Speaking Out*, he is one of the most troubled about his homeland. Jews have no business in Germany, he says; but here we are, and both we and the Germans have to live with the fact. Schneider is well aware that his choice not just to live in Germany, but to become a German citizen (a decision he made as a young adult) was made entirely of his own free will; yet it does not sit easily. He agonizes over his identity, his loyalties. "Okay, we are German citizens," he says, "so what should we (Jews) do?"

Schneider himself has no answer to that question, although he feels that Jews should take an active part in their own history and not act—or rather react—as potential victims. No author would be able to agree more fervently on this point than Michael Wolffsohn, whose attitudes are in almost all other respects very different from Schneider's. Indeed, very different from most other Jews living in Germany, for Wolffsohn views himself as a living fossil: a German-Jewish patriot. A Jew with strong bonds both to Judaism and to Israel (where he was born of German parents and later served in the armed forces), Wolffsohn's national feelings are strongest with regard to Germany. Germany is in the true sense of the word his fatherland, German is his mother tongue. And he considers it quite natural to love his native land, to experience an inwardly (as opposed to outwardly) directed nationalism.

By no means all of the *Speaking Out* authors discuss in detail their own complex relationship to Germany, for by no means all of the authors have written autobiographical essays. However, a general preoccupation with the subject is evident throughout the book. Rafael Seligmann suggests that the post-Auschwitz generation has decided in favor of living in Germany out of inertia. We are here, he says, because German is our language and culture, we have German friends and spouses, we work and live in the country. We are Germans, whether we—or anyone else, for that matter—like it or not. And, he adds, we have an important function: to sound the alarm whenever there is a need to make people aware of dangers at hand. In other words, Seligmann attributes to the Jews the active role that Schneider wishes for them.

One of the first questions put to Jews living in Germany by the rest of the world (including non-Jewish Germans in Germany) concerns anti-Semitism. Isn't anti-Semitism still a serious problem in Germany today, and how do the Jews deal with it? There is a ready answer to the first part of the question: anti-Semitism exists everywhere, even in countries with no Jews (in Japan, for example); at the same time, anti-Semitism is no more prevalent in Germany than elsewhere. Depending on which polling organization is consulted, anti-Semitism is either at a postwar low in Germany (the Allensbach Institute), or on the increase (the Emnid Institute)—but either way, there appears to be less anti-Semitism in Germany than in such countries as France or even the United States. However, when it comes to Germany, arguments based on facts and figures are usually countered by emotion; in the country responsible for the Holocaust, anti-Semitism takes on a special dimension, it is far more threatening and far less tolerable than it is "elsewhere."

How Jews in Germany deal with the problem is more complicated, and anti-Semitism is another recurrent theme in the contributions to this book. It haunts the authors, who talk of personal as well as generalized experience. What comes through is often a sense of genuine unease, which, however, seems more based on mind-set and memory (firsthand or inherited) than on present reality. Ignatz Bubis (as I have already mentioned, himself a survivor and the spokesman for the Jew-

18

ish Community in Germany) views the situation most dispassionately. Anti-Semitism has never ceased to exist in Germany, he maintains, but it has not become any stronger in recent years and, contrary to popular belief, has not been affected by unification. What worries Ignatz Bubis is qualitative rather than quantitative; anti-Semitism today has become more respectable, and anti-Semites who until lately kept their opinions to themselves now have no qualms about admitting them. This increasing respectability of anti-Semitic attitudes is noted by other authors, but Richard Schneider for one is not entirely unhappy about it, because it "at least gives us the advantage of knowing right away who our enemies are."

For Henryk Broder, anti-Semitism needs to be defined. Where does it begin, he asks, what yardstick are we to use? If anti-Semitism starts at Auschwitz, and to be recognized as an anti-Semite, a person has to have murder—or even genocide—in mind, then there are precious few anti-Semites around. But if we lower the standards, so to speak, and apply the label to those well-educated, well-bred members of the community who "merely" wish to exclude Jews from social life, then the picture looks very different. And it looks even more different if we include all those who harbor anti-Semitic views without even knowing it. Broder takes an almost perverse delight in pouncing on seemingly innocent statements which could, with a bit of bad will, be interpreted as anti-Semitic, but he makes a valid point. Where indeed does anti-Semitism start?

Rafael Seligmann does not concern himself with definitions. Like Broder, he quotes the recent Emnid poll which finds that more than one third of all Germans hold anti-Semitic opinions (insofar as 39 percent of those surveyed considered that the Jews exploit the Holocaust for their own ends). Jews in Germany need a thick skin to survive, announces Seligmann, who nevertheless acknowledges that anti-Semitism in the German population is "no more and no less than in comparable countries." In fact, Seligmann appears to be less concerned about anti-Semitism than about philo-

Semitism, which he sees as just as discriminatory. The philo-Semites, driven by feelings of guilt, insist on viewing the Jews as morally superior beings. This, of course, imposes something of a burden on those Jews who feel they have to live up to the elevated image. Jewish literature in postwar Germany has suffered greatly from philo-Semitism, claims Seligmann, because it has been "sterilized of hate;" Jews dare not give expression to their anger at the harm done to them in the past by the Germans for fear of disappointing their self-appointed "friends."

Yael Grözinger, still in her early twenties and the youngest author in this book, is also disturbed about anti- and philo-Semitism, which she sees as two sides of a coin. In offering her examples of both, she makes the point that no matter how negatively or positively they are viewed, Jews in Germany are "special," if only because they are inevitably viewed in the one way or the other. They are also "special" because there are so few of them, so each individual becomes the representative of the entire Jewish population in Germany and is expected to be an expert on every aspect of Jewish life. Cilly Kugelmann goes a step further; she refers to what she calls a "labelling process that has taken place since the war, whereby every single Jew has come to be looked upon as a symbolic representative of the six million Jews who were murdered and the few who survived . . . According to this role, every Jew is an expert on Jewish religion, the history of National Socialism and the Holocaust; he or she is duty-bound to account for, and accept responsibility for, the policy of every Israeli government."

If each and every Jew in Germany is a symbolic representative of all Jews past and present, then there are anywhere between 50,000 and 60,000 representatives currently residing in the country (which has a population of 81 million). Approximately 43,000 are registered members of the Jewish Community; the rest are not members, for whatever reason, and their numbers can only be guessed at. This is one reason for the widely different figures given by the various authors (figures which I have made no attempt to harmonize). Indeed, the authors rarely agree on any numbers, be they of the size of the Jewish population before the war (between 500,000 and 600,000), or of the number of Jews who ended up on German soil as Displaced Persons after 1945 (between 200,000 and 300,000), or the number of immigrants from the former Soviet Union who have arrived in Germany as so-called quota-refugees since 1989 (between 10,000 and 20,000).

The last statistic is particularly obscure, since nobody is quite sure how many of the ex-Soviet immigrants who claim to be Jewish are, in fact, Jewish—and as Wolf Biermann and Elvira Grözinger make clear in different contexts, determining who is and who is not Jewish is often a matter of interpretation. Moreover, many of these so-called Russians Jews (a misnomer, says Peter Ambros, who still uses the term) are married to non-Jews and have families, so the counting becomes even more confused. Sofia Mill, herself a recent ex-Soviet Jewish immigrant, reckons that in many of the families entering Germany on the Jewish ticket, for every "half-Jew" there are four to five non-Jews. But however many ex-Soviet Jews there are, there is general agreement that they already constitute a sizeable percentage of all of the Jews living in Germany. The policy of the German government to allow ex-Soviet Jews to enter the country on a quota is viewed by Rafael Seligmann as totally inadequate, by Igor Reichlin as generous and by Sofia Mill as vaguely suspect; the fact remains that no other non-Germans are able to settle in Germany on a similar basis, since Germany continues to insist that it is not an immigration country. The ex-Soviet Jews are therefore de facto a privileged group. If they continue to migrate to Germany at the same rate over the coming years (and there is no reason to suppose that they will not, despite Rafael Seligmann's claim that they have been put off by incidents of xenophobia), Micha Brumlik and Igor Reichlin both estimate that by the end of this century, they will have raised the number of Jews in Germany to around 100,000—at which point they will constitute a clear majority of the Jewish population.

No wonder, then, that a number of authors have something to say about this growing population. Because of its sheer size, and because it is culturally very different from the existing Jewish population, it defies easy integration. On the contrary, in cities such as Berlin, where it is concentrated, and in communities where the Russian Jews make up almost the entire membership, it is already having a considerable impact. Many of the newcomers have no basic knowledge of Judaism; at best, as Uri Kaufmann puts it, the oldest age group will have some recollection of Jewish customs which their parents cultivated, and some may still know some Yiddish. Sofia Mill agrees; Russian Jews have no Jewish religious identity, she maintains, and some of them quickly lose interest in the Jewish communities they gravitate to when they first arrive. Others, however, are already looking for an active role in community politics, not for religious reasons, but because they need an outlet for their energy. It is these immigrants who will challenge the establishment; Micha Brumlik anticipates that the Russian Jews will be a contributing factor in the relaxing of the religious Orthodoxy currently practiced in almost all of the communities.

Any deviation from this Orthodox variant of Judaism still constitutes something of a revolution, since the powers-that-be in the Jewish Community consider that Jewry in Germany is too small to allow religious pluralism. But even Ignatz Bubis admits that within the united (Orthodox) communities, not all members share the same Orthodox religious outlook; some consider themselves to be Reform or liberal. Uri Kaufmann goes much further; he claims that "Orthodox families (in Germany) are few and far between," indeed, that many Jews are essentially lax in their personal religious behavior, but since they have to defend their presence in Germany, they pay lip service to a rigid form of religion. Both Uri Kaufmann and Micha Brumlik see new "liberal" approaches as inevitable (and welcome), and report that independent groups are already forming throughout the country to explore new ways of dealing with religion in a changing society.

If religion does not provide the Jews with their sense of identity, what then does? This key question is of course not confined to Jews in Germany, but in this case, the country most certainly plays a major role. The mere fact of living in the land of the Holocaust automatically reinforces the identity of anyone who lays claim to being Jewish, for whatever reason and to whatever degree. It is not a question of being Jewish in the eyes of Jewish law, of being in any way religious, or even of keeping tradition. Being Jewish in Germany is perceiving oneself or being perceived as different, special, if only by virtue of "belonging to" the victims rather than to the perpetrators.

Rafael Seligmann is worried about this negative identification. Judaism in Germany is in danger of defining itself as a community of victims and of being regarded as such by friend and foe alike, he says; and while he does not think that this "Holocaust fixation" endangers large Jewish communities in other countries such as the United States, Britain or France, he sees it as destructive in Germany. Hanno Loewy, on the other hand, takes issue with Seligmann. For him, the Holocaust does not confirm identity ("in the continuity of the role of the victim") but "generates at best a 'sense of community' only because it represents a common problem for Jewish identity."

What does it mean to be a Jew in Germany? asks Richard Schneider, and answers as a child of his generation: "Nowhere in the world do Jews live with such serious ruptures in their soul as they do in Germany, nowhere is their identity as questionable as it is here, since for those of us born (in Germany) after the war it already means being 'German' again to some extent."

Wolf Biermann talks at length about his own identity, "half Jew-brat, half goy." For the Jews, not a Jew, for the Nazis, a Jew; "I am not Jewish and have always been Jewish," says this man who spent 23 years in East Germany, where Jews were systematically stripped of their Jewish identity—*entjudet* or de-Jewified. "The Nazis wiped out the Jewish people—but the Stalinists preferred to liquidate everything that was Jewish in the Jews."

Nevertheless, Jalda Rebling, a member of the small East Berlin Jewish Community, managed to escape being *entjudet*. On the contrary, even before the East German regime "discovered an interest in all things Jewish" in the late 1980s, she was a singer of Yiddish songs, a performer with an international reputation. Rebling is in constant search of a *heimishkeit* which she herself says is lost forever; but she remains dedicated to preserving Yiddish and the culture it represents.

Preserving Jewish culture and history is particularly important and particularly difficult in Germany. As long as it was uncertain whether the Jews had a future in the country (and it was not until the 1980s that the Jews stopped sitting on packed suitcases and acknowledged that they were around to stay), there was no pressing need to make their history available to a wider audience. That need obviously exists today, although as Cilly Kugelmann explains, Jewish museums present their own problems. The German-Jewish relationship, which has gone through a number of stages since the end of the war, plays a major role here. Many Jews themselves are ambivalent towards such museums, since the majority originally come from eastern Europe and have little interest in the history of German Jews. Since the museums are funded by public money through the municipality or state, the Jews tend to regard them as "German" institutions. And for a complex of reasons, many Jews in Germany prefer "to avoid places where their fate and their history are put on public display or made a subject of discussion."

Just as Jewish museums sprung up in Germany in the 1980s, so too did other institutions dedicated to the preservation of Jewish history and culture. Maintaining a proper archive system, claims Peter Honigmann, has something to do

24

with being firmly rooted. Throughout the years that the Jews considered themselves to be in transit, passing through Germany on their way to somewhere else, the written material documenting their past was sent out of the country and stored in Israel and the United States. This situation has now changed; material pertaining to Judaism and the Jews is being collected and made available for research in Germany and a central archive has been established in Heidelberg.

The 1980s proved to be a turning point in the postwar history of Jews in Germany. With the subtle change in attitude towards Germany as their home and the consequent feeling of being more settled, the Jews acquired a new self-confidence, a new willingness to raise their voices when they felt the need, and in general to make their opinions heard. At the same time, the 1980s saw a change in the attitude of a number of Germans towards their own history; a desire in some circles to relegate the Holocaust to history and declare it a closed chapter became apparent, as did a less widespread desire to universalize the horror of the Nazi period and view it in historical context. The Jews were outraged, and on three occasions in particular took a firm stand: when Chancellor Kohl invited then President Reagan to honor the war dead (including SS officers) at Bitburg★; when an attempt was made to stage the Rainer Werner Fassbinder★ play *Garbage, The City and Death*; and when the historian Ernst Nolte★ tried to relativize the Holocaust. That these episodes are to this day considered significant can be judged by how often they are mentioned by the authors in *Speaking Out*.

The 1980s are already history, a new century is only a few years away. As the postwar Jewish community in Germany becomes increasingly settled, its concerns are becoming increasingly internal. Whereas in earlier years, it would have done its best to keep its "family" affairs to itself, today they are often played out in front of the German media. In Berlin, a small Orthodox independent congregation, "Adass Yisroel," is fighting a public battle with the established Jewish Commu-

nity over certain legal rights it claims it has. Both Uri Kaufmann and Micha Brumlik mention the independent community in connection with growing religious pluralism; they do
not (and could not within the context of their chapters) discuss the power and money issues involved. Suffice it to say
that the complex controversy occupies news and commentary
columns of national newspapers, and the offer made by *Speaking Out* author Ernst Cramer to mediate between the antag-
onistic parties was reported in the press and could be seen on
television.

Indeed, given the size of the Jewish population in Germany, it is remarkable how much media time and space is devoted to it. Certainly, shocking events such as the bombing of
the synagogue in Lübeck or acts of vandalism at concentration
camp sites (Sachsenhausen and Buchenwald) make the head-
lines; but the national media also carry stories on less dramatic
happenings such as the re-inauguration of Germany's largest
synagogue in Frankfurt, or even minor squabbles between
prominent Jews. For better or worse, the small Jewish community is very much in the public eye, far more so than the
vastly bigger Muslim community, for example. The authors in
Speaking Out have different attitudes towards the German fascination with the Jews in their midst, but many of the public
figures and professional writers among them (Bubis, Biermann, Broder, Giordano, Seligmann, Wolffsohn) are anything
but media-shy. When they raise their voices, they are not unhappy when they are heard.

Speaking Out makes no claim to be a comprehensive survey
of Jewish life in Germany today. As I started out by saying, its
primary raison d'être is to show that there *is* Jewish life in
contemporary Germany, that this Jewish life is viable and becoming ever more firmly established, both in its own consciousness and—perhaps as a consequence—in the consciousness of non-Jewish Germans. It is my hope that this book will
contribute to a better understanding of the undeniably complex Jews-in-Germany situation, not only on the part of those

who do not always react with tolerance to the Jews that live here, but also on the part of all those who are simply curious about the small but significant and above all evolving Jewish population and its environment.

On the Way to Pluralism?
Jewish Communities in Germany Today

by Uri R. Kaufmann

In the not so distant future, the majority of the German population will no longer be Christian. Only 43 million of some 80 million Germans are still members of the Protestant or Catholic church. Thirty-five million are listed as having no confession. Around 1.4 million are Muslims, most of them Turks, and several hundred thousand belong to free churches or sects.

In the various European countries, relations between the state and religion are regulated in very different ways. Whereas in France there has been a strict separation of church and state since 1905, this is not the arrangement that exists in Germany. The two main churches are constituted as corporate entities under public law, which means that the state collects church tax on their behalf and usually subsidizes their social welfare activities (in the State of Baden-Württemberg, for example, this subsidy amounts to 40 percent of the church tax). Church representatives have a voice in the selection of candidates to fill the professorial positions of the respective divinity schools. A well-publicized case was that of the Swiss Catholic professor Hans Küng, whose authorization to teach was rescinded by the church. As a form of compensation, the state created an Institute of Ecumenical Theology in Tübingen just for him. These costly training facilities are also paid for by the state or, to be more precise, by the individual German states. When someone registers with the German authorities as a member of one of the two churches, church tax is automatically withheld by the German tax authorities. In Baden-Württemberg, church tax is equivalent to eight percent of income tax. People can leave the church by submitting a written declaration to their district court.

The Jewish communities are also included in this governmental framework. From 1919 to 1933—in other words, during the period when the Weimar constitution was in force—this legal tradition applied to them as well, and after the Shoah★ this situation was restored. As public-law entities, religious denominations have the right to appoint delegates to charitable associations, government foundations and certain public-sector bodies. This explains the anomalous situation whereby a Jewish community with no more than a few thousand or even a few hundred members in a given state can appoint representatives to the boards of the publicly funded broadcasting stations, whereas the Muslim community, which may be a hundred times larger, cannot.

On the face of it, religious affiliation in Germany is quasi-compulsory. Anyone who is not registered as a member of a denomination is regarded by the state as having no religion. Prior to the Shoah, the Jewish communities in Germany were organized as so-called "united communities." There was room for all three branches of Judaism under one roof: Orthodox, Conservative and Reform. As we know, in the mid-19th century, these three German-Jewish approaches to Judaism had an impact on Jews in the United States; indeed, American Jewry is still organized along these lines today.

Large urban German-Jewish communities used to have several synagogues, with one or more serving each current of Judaism. In Frankfurt at the end of the 19th century, for example, Rabbi Marcus Horowitz held fast to Orthodox practice in his own synagogue, yet was not fazed in the least by the fact that Reform ritual (with an organ!) was practiced in other synagogues in the same community. Seligmann Bär Bamberger, the famous "Würzburg Rav," spoke out in favor of keeping the religious community together and was opposed to separatism. However, some of the Orthodoxy did not want to support any non-Orthodox groups. In 1851, for example, Samson Raphael Hirsch founded a separate, independent community in Frankfurt, which had to build and finance its own institutions (synagogue, cemetery, etc.) from the ground up. There were similar "separatist" communities in Mainz, Darmstadt, Wiesbaden, Karlsruhe, Berlin and a few other places, but their membership made up only a small percentage of all Jews in Germany. The majority of them were members of both congregations, against Hirsch's will.

After the Shoah, Jews from other places found themselves living in areas of the former German Reich under Allied occupation. Most of them came from eastern Europe and were "Displaced Persons," the majority of whom wanted to move on to some other place. In 1947, there were probably about 200,000 Jews living in Germany. Ninety percent of them migrated to Palestine, or the young state of Israel, or went to the United States. Only very few Jews of German origin and culture came back—an estimated 3,000 to 4,000. In 1956, many Hungarian Jewish families moved to Germany, and in 1968 some came from what was then Czechoslovakia. In addition to a Romanian contingent, a group of Israelis can also be found in or around most Jewish communities in Germany today. Thus, the composition of the communities is extremely heterogeneous. This may be one reason why it is often difficult to find a common denominator in community affairs.

It was very hard for many who had been persecuted by the Nazi regime to build up an existence of their own from nothing. Those who were immediate victims of Nazi persecution in their youth did not have any regular schooling or vocational training. They owned nothing. Many of them got into the restaurant business after 1945. The Allied forces were all in favor of granting bar and restaurant licenses to Jewish entrepreneurs. Running such businesses was the predominant occupation among Jews in the 1950s and 1960s, and Jewish-owned restaurants are still common in many places today. This "reconstruc-tion-era" generation then made it possible for their children to do what they had not been able to do themselves—complete their schooling and, in many cases, go on to college or university as well.

Today (1994), the great majority of the Jews in Germany— probably two-thirds of some 40,000—live in six big cities— Berlin, Frankfurt, Munich, Düsseldorf, Cologne and Ham-burg.

The all-powerful "founding fathers" of the 1950s now began talking about restoring the "united community," but in reality there was no longer any tripartite division of religious currents; in fact, the overwhelming majority was secular in outlook. Only in Berlin were two rabbinates set up with one synagogue each, one of them liberal and the other Orthodox. However, the "liberal" synagogue in Pestalozzistrasse is more comparable to a right-of-center Conservative synagogue in the United States: women cantors and rabbis are not per-mitted to date (July 1994); men and women are seated sepa-rately during the service and prayers are read in Hebrew.

Whereas in Switzerland rabbis are elected by the members of the congregation, in Germany the Executive Board or Re-gional Council has the final say. There has been a noticeable preference for rabbis with Orthodox leanings. At present, only one of the 12 "officially" installed rabbis is liberal and only one Conservative. Frankfurt recently even went so far as to call in a Hasidic rabbi from Bene Beraq (Israel) for what is considered, after all, a very secular community. Munich has three Orthodox rabbis, but they have not been able to raise the level of religious involvement: the synagogue in Reichen-bachstrasse is poorly attended.

To the outside—again with the exception of Berlin—all of the congregations in Germany give the appearance of being Orthodox. Up to a point, there is a tendency in every Jewish Diaspora community to give the impression of being more re-ligious than it really is. In Germany, however, the contrast seems to be more extreme than elsewhere. Orthodox families here are few and far between.

In addition, those who re-established the Jewish communities in Germany usually took a tight hold of the reins. In some cases, they functioned as cantor, teacher, manager and president, all in one, and did not prepare anyone else to succeed them in even one of these functions. They often held on to their positions until they were very old, and this is still the case today: It was not unusual then, nor is it now, to find octogenarians holding office in Jewish organizations in Germany. Their style of leadership was often very authoritarian but they had acquired such an important status through their relationships with municipal councils and state governments that a majority of the communities' members always voted them in again. A very dim view was taken of opposition within the community. For that reason, and because of the monolithic-Orthodox image projected to the outside (with no basis in real life), one is tempted to describe the prevailing attitude in the communities as a "siege mentality." However, this attitude is no longer so much in evidence, if at all, among the younger generation of today. Having grown up in Germany, their socialization has been different from that of their parents. Moreover, they are familiar with the way things work in Jewish communities elsewhere, such as the pluralistic American Jewish community. They have made an effort to publish non-conformist periodicals. The quarterly *Frankfurter Jüdische Nachrichten* and the magazine *Babylon*, both of which are put together by a Frankfurt circle of Jewish intellectuals (Micha Brumlik, Cilly Kugelmann, Doron Kiesel and Dan Diner, among others), have lasted longer than any of the other new periodicals so far.

Now that the community institutions have been well and truly established, community members have more time to focus on issues and values. Within the space of a single year (1993/94), Jews who were not satisfied with the Orthodox religious service have formed groups in Frankfurt, Hannover,

Oldenburg, Regensburg and Heidelberg, the purpose of which is to look for new approaches.

A countercurrent is the—in religious terms—rightward shift which is characteristic of many Jewish communities. In this age of esotericism, in which so many people are turning to the mystical religions of Asia in search of meaning, there are also a few Jews who evade the difficult task of coming to terms with the Modern Age by turning to fundamentalism for spiritual guidance. However, followers of this current in Germany find it too strenuous to practice Orthodox religion in their day-to-day lives, and this has led to the peculiar phenomenon of "non-observant Orthodoxy." In Germany, there may be an additional factor involved which serves to exaggerate this overall trend. The early 1980s saw an intensification of interest in coming to terms with the Shoah, a process which led many American and Israeli Jews to question the legitimacy of Jewish life in Germany with renewed force. Young Jews from Germany are often asked about it and manoeuvered into a defensive position, which can, in turn, engender feelings of guilt. Some Jews in Germany then think they must compensate for their own alleged "illegitimacy" by paying lip service to an especially rigid religious attitude. In other words, they want a full-length Orthodox religious service, including the re-introduction of passages that were done away with in Germany as long as 170 years ago (*"B'rich sh'mei . . . Yekum purkan . . ."*)—but it is too much trouble for them to get to the synagogue on time on the morning of the Sabbath, not to mention getting up before daybreak on weekdays to say the *shacharit*, the morning prayer. Even in big communities in Germany, minyan men have to be paid just to get the necessary quorum for weekday services. So, envoys of the Lubavitch movement find sympathizers in Frankfurt and Munich, but not very many of them are willing to practice Orthodox Judaism in their daily lives.

The biggest problem right now is the integration of the Russian Jews who have recently immigrated to Germany—

numbering some 15,000 by the summer of 1994. As far as the religious aspect is concerned, however, many of those who have come to Germany have no basic knowledge of Judaism. At best, the oldest age group will have some recollection of Jewish customs which their parents still cultivated back in the 1930s. This group also still knows some Yiddish. On the whole, the newcomers are products of a secular Russian culture. They play a passive rather than an active role within the inner-Jewish discussion. This has put the communities in Germany under even more pressure because they were often unable to provide the basis for proper religious instruction for their children even before the arrival of the newcomers. There was a huge lack of qualified Jewish teachers throughout western Europe. However, it is a role which still carries little prestige, even today; careers as doctors and lawyers or in private industry are much more attractive for the great majority of young Jews. Teachers from Israel were often hired but they were not able to teach the children very much and also, in some cases, had no background in educational skills. There were also language problems, since, after all, the older generation of "yekkes," German-speaking Jews, is gradually dying out. So, there was a high turnover of teachers.

The proposition made by Rabbi Nathan Peter Levinson in 1971 to promote the establishment of a "Center for Jewish Studies" under Jewish authority was a positive and important step towards alleviating this deficiency. The institution was established in 1979, in partnership with the old and venerated University of Heidelberg. It has come a long way since then, and currently offers 40 different courses per semester (with a faculty of 13 teachers), making it the broadest Jewish Studies program in Germany. With an enrollment of 146 students (winter semester 1994/95), it is the second largest Jewish Studies institution in Germany. In December 1994, the State of Baden-Württemberg approved the establishment of a doctoral degree program. The Center's plans to provide teacher-training as a supplement to the "Master's degree in Jewish

Studies" are now underway. The level of interest on the part of non-Jews has been so high that only 19 of the 96 majors are Jewish. However, if all of the 26 Jewish graduates and students find their way into the communities, that would already be quite a big step forward for Jewish education in Germany. At present, 16 Jewish graduates and students are already working in youth programs and religious instruction. Former students of the institution include the current chief rabbi of Prague, Karol Sidon, the most prominent figure to have received his basic training in Heidelberg and been ordained in Israel. It is also interesting to find that inquiries are coming in from eastern Europe, or that scholars from Slovakia, for example, are using the research library, which has a respectable 35,000 resources. There are also already students from the new eastern states of Germany, from Austria, Poland and Russia, as well as Jewish exchange students in the field of German studies from the English-speaking world (Canada and Britain), who were attracted by the special atmosphere of Heidelberg. Like the much larger Christian divinity schools, the Jewish college is funded primarily by the federal government and the states. The fact is, this college offers the Jewish community in the German-speaking world, including Austria (6,000 Jews) and Switzerland (17,500 Jews), an opportunity to receive a state-funded university education in Jewish studies—an opportunity which even the much larger Jewish community in France, with its some 500,000 members, can only dream of.

The religious denominations which are officially recognized by the state are required to organize their communities in state-level associations. These centralized organizations, in turn, are in charge of distributing the tax revenue that is collected by the state from members of the respective denominations. In the regional councils of the Jewish communities— as elsewhere—this sometimes leads to a disagreeable tug-of-war over who gets what piece of the pie. Moreover, feuding based on the personal interests of individual families does little to promote the general good. More often than not, the style of negotiation is rough: the simple fact of the matter is, people who have developed a thick skin in the business world behave the same way when seated on the boards of Jewish communities.

The regional councils send delegates to the Central Council of Jews in Germany. This council is divided into a parliament, the so-called "Council Assembly," and the smaller directorate, a kind of executive committee which meets at more frequent intervals. The Central Council is headed by the chairman of the directorate, a post currently occupied by Ignatz Bubis, who is also chairman of the Frankfurt Jewish Community. Unlike his predecessor, Heinz Galinski, who was politically neutral and had the manner of a stern, unapproachable admonisher, Bubis belongs to a political party (the Free Democratic Party, FDP), is very favorably disposed to the media, and also makes effective use of them as a spokesman, even on political issues of a general nature, such as government policy on political refugees. The Rabbinical Conference, which is attached to the Central Council, is responsible for religious matters. Theoretically, the Conference is supposed to include all rabbis appointed by the Jewish communities and regional associations. However, there are differences of opinion here as well, and the body has refused to recognize a few of the rabbis who are working in the German communities. A rabbinical court with three members (*bet din*) was recently founded, and has been approved by the Israeli Chief Rabbinate.

In comparison to the situation in the United States, this centralist organizational structure seems extremely monolithic. In reality, however, changes have been taking place beneath the surface over the last few years. In East Berlin, at a time when the German Democratic Republic still existed, one family re-established the Orthodox separatist congregation which had formerly existed there, "Adass Yisroel," initially with support from Israel. They retained a clever lawyer, Lothar de Maizière, who later became prime minister of the collapsing GDR. Important pieces of real estate that had once been held by "Adass Yisroel" were returned to the congregation, and today it has a sizable income from rents. For the most part, it is financially independent. This community did not want to merge with the Jewish Community in West Berlin or to affiliate with the Central Council, and made clever propaganda by opening a café on Oranienburgerstrasse, the former Jewish center, as well as providing intensive assistance and services to Russian immigrants. In October 1994, the Berlin Senate gave formal recognition to this independent community, to the great dismay of the "established" Berlin Jewish Community. In another non-affiliated initiative in East Berlin, the children of Jewish Communist functionaries have formed their own cultural organization. They are now trying to learn about Jewish history and culture on their own, and they also publish their own newsletter. For the sake of completeness, it should be mentioned that according to official figures, there were about 400 registered Jewish community members living in the former East German state prior to 1989.

In the western part of Berlin, an opposition group has been gaining ground in the community, and won almost half of the votes in the last elections. This, too, is a sign that the internal polity of the Jewish Community is moving towards pluralism. A few years have already passed since the Jewish Community in the city of Giessen chose to withdraw from the Central Council. Some communities in Bavaria have also resigned from the state association. It is hard to say whether the Central Council's claim to represent the community as a whole will be eroded any further.

On that note, it should be pointed out that there is also a group of Jews, estimated at over 10,000, who are either not registered as Jews with the German authorities or have NATO status as members of the U.S. armed forces and do not have to register as legal residents with the German authorities. In the first case, the reason for not registering as a Jew has often been that people did not want to pay any church tax. As far as many Israelis are concerned, it can be assumed that they did not state their religion as "Jewish"—and were especially reluctant to do so for German authorities. Many of them do not consider their emigration from Israel as final, and registering with a Jewish community might destroy this illusion.

In any case, it can be said that the beginnings of a form of pluralism, both religious and political, have been developing over the last four years at the grassroots level. This process is impeded by the fact that the Jewish religious community is interlocked with the state. In my opinion, the provision of funding by and via the state has also contributed to a reduction in the level of involvement and motivation in the Jewish communities: donations are very difficult to come by, since people have the feeling that they "already gave at the office"— by paying church tax. On the other hand, it is only because of state funding that new synagogues have been built in many places, Jewish schools have been opened and the Heidelberg Center for Jewish Studies was instituted. And without the government's support, the communities and the Central Welfare Board of the Jews in Germany would not be able to offer the comprehensive social services that they in fact provide for older and younger members of the community, and for the Russian immigrants in particular.

Auschwitz—and Life!
Why I Have Remained in Germany

by Ralph Giordano

1.

Yes, why?

My family and I were liberated from the illegal existence we were leading in the darkness of a cellar in Hamburg by the Eighth Army under Field Marshal Montgomery on May 4, 1945. When we crawled out of it—my father, mother, my two brothers and I—we only very vaguely resembled human beings. If the "desert rats" had not made it to the Elbe until just a few days later, we would not have lived to see them, but would have died of starvation. Our lives had long since become a race between the "final solution" and "final victory" by the opponents of Hitler's Germany. It had been quite obvious to all of us before liberation that, if we lived to see it, we would leave Germany, would shake its blood-stained dust from our feet as quickly as we could.

As of about 1938, we began calling them "the Germans"— "we" had nothing more to do with "them." And we still felt this way after World War II broke out, but with a slight difference—we now felt that we were part of the Allies, of the coalition against Hitler, our potential liberators. They were our home and our hope. There was no other.

But there is a prologue to all this, and an epilogue.

2.

We started to become isolated immediately after Hitler came to power at the end of January 1933.

As early as April of that year, on our first day of enrollment in secondary school we were already being divided up into "Aryan" and "non-Aryan" pupils—an unforgettable experience, being weeded out from the others on that very first day, putting an early end to the feeling of being equal among equals—we were branded, contemptible, inferior.

As time went on, and in line with Nazi racist policy, this experience was followed by all the stations of persecution, which not only included our being stripped of rights by the state, such as being barred from certain professions, being interrogated by the Gestapo, being expelled from school, and being faced with endless lists of prohibitions, but also anti-Semitic actions on the part of private individuals, with people being physically abused, denounced or terrorized by hatemail. Eventually, based on a realistic assessment of the system which ruled amidst the jubilant cries of the vast majority of the population, our own lives came to be ruled by a single, overwhelming fear—the fear of a violent death which could come at any time. So that, finally, we decided to avoid such an eventuality by going underground . . .

I am trying to convey here in a few brief words the unimaginable state of terror which I have described in more detail in *The Bertinis*, my thinly disguised autobiographical saga of a Hamburg family and the persecution they suffered.

In other words, up to the time of liberation, the inevitable had inevitably come to pass—we were completely uprooted, politically, psychologically, socially, and mentally.

3.

Which brings me to the crux of the matter, namely, the question of belonging.

When I was denied that feeling of belonging because of my Jewish descent for the first time on that April morning at school in 1933, I was ten years old, an extremely impressionable age. The exclusion showed which way the new wind was blowing, although the full implications of the dangers it bode were not yet apparent. And the first, severe internal wounds that were about to come were not inflicted so much from the top, by the state, but came from a different, unofficial direction where one would have least expected them—which made them all the more painful.

Like the morning of that summer day in 1934, when I came up to my buddies in the same cheerful way I always had, kids I had known ever since childhood, had grown up with, people my own age, only to be greeted with the curt and hostile call: "We don't play with Jews—you're not our friend anymore!"

I will never forget how it felt to have friendship and affection withdrawn so abruptly and without warning, even if I live to be as old as Methuselah. Even today, when I am free to decide who I want for a friend, and people tend to seek my friendship, even today that moment of 60 years ago is still so vivid in my mind that my hair stands on end whenever I think of it.

When the Nuremberg Laws* to "Protect German Blood and German Honor" were proclaimed and enacted in September 1935, it was already quite clear to me, a 12 year-old at the time, that I did not want to belong to the people who did not allow me to belong to them, not for anything in the world. And when, after eons of being in power (because that is how long those 12 years seemed to me at the time, even if they amount to just a sixth of my life so far), they were finally beaten on land, at sea and in the air, I felt not only that the

41

Nazi system was my mortal enemy but also a sense of alienation from "the Germans" as such, a feeling so profound that it can hardly be described. The only ones who were not affected by it, really, were those who had remained personal friends, the helpers and life-savers. I regarded all the others, the anonymous ones, the unknown millions, as my adversaries, from the ones who went along with the system to the political murderers of individuals and masses.

Attempting to achieve some sense of belonging when one is filled with feelings such as these—can there be anything more difficult in the life of a human being, especially if one is young? But something embedded in my biography was already guiding me, even then, without my being aware of it yet, something which had taken hold of me and yet was beyond me to define at that point—the umbilical cord to the Holocaust, which I had only escaped by chance, the "law" of my life, as I call it. What I mean is the internal bond to the world of the victims, those who had been murdered, the "compass of Auschwitz"—and the lesson to be learned from it: "Never again!"

However, the center of this struggle was here—in Germany—whether I liked it or not.

4.

And more often than not I did not.

Survivors of the Nazi policy of race and the genocide committed against the Jews in German-occupied Europe during World War II have *two* burdens to bear, and both of them blocked the emergence of a new sense of belonging.

The *first* of these burdens is the memory of the atrocities experienced from 1933 to 1945.

The half-century which has gone by since liberation has been time enough to find out that time does not heal anything! On the contrary—the further away we get from the

42

events of the past, the closer we get to the images of horror inside us, the more vivid the details become, the shorter the intervals between increasingly horrible nightmares—delayed syndromes of many survivors of the Shoah★. Today I know they will last a lifetime.

Now, add to this first burden a second one, namely the stigma of German postwar history—the almost complete exoneration of the Nazi perpetrators!

With few exceptions, which, moreover, are to the credit of Allied military courts, they not only got off scot-free, but were even able to carry on their careers as if nothing had happened. Within the borders of what was West Germany, the biggest crime known to history, with millions and millions of victims, who were killed like insects—*behind* the frontlines no less—was followed by the biggest "rehabilitation" operation for perpetrators that has ever existed. It was only natural for those who had been the experts in destruction prior to 1945 to become the expert architects of reconstruction, of the "economic miracle" which followed thereafter. Indeed, the industrial, military and bureaucratic elite in West Germany well into the 1970s was virtually identical to the elite under Hitler—perpetual winners.

Prosecution under the German criminal justice system never amounted to anything more than a token attempt at atonement, but still took an enormous amount of time and effort. Since 1958, for 37 years, in other words, there has been an almost uninterrupted flow of court cases against Nazi perpetrators, including mammoth ordeals such as the trials that dragged on for years in Frankfurt and Düsseldorf against the guards at Auschwitz and Maidanek. An endless string of defendants were charged with murder and tons of files and documentation were plowed through in the process. Yet, anyone who monitored these proceedings over a longer period of time, for decades, as I did, soon realized that the only ones in the docks of the West German courts came almost exclusively from the lowest-level links in the chain of production-line serial killing and mass murder, of genocide. Those on trial were the "little clerks" of the administrative massacre (which was then treated with inordinate leniency by a postwar legal system that had never been cleansed of its Nazi elements, and with a leniency which contrasted sharply with the harsh sentences that were meted out to left-wing terrorists). But their superiors, the organizers of Auschwitz and everything which this name symbolizes and calls to mind, the real murderers who had run the machinery of destruction from their desks in the Reich Central Security Office, were never even charged, let alone convicted. Nor were any of the Nazi system's cold-blooded judges—in spite of 32,000 documented cases of people who were sentenced to death for political reasons—none of them was ever duly sentenced by a West German court, not a single one. It was no different with Hitler's diplomats, the leaders of Germany's armaments-based economy and high-ranking military figures after 1945. And if any of them were actually put behind bars by the Allied courts, they were released by the mid-1950s at the latest: They had been exculpated by the Cold War, given that Germany was now sought as an ally in view of the global rivalry which had sprung up between the superpowers, the United States and the Soviet Union—the fault line of which ran through the middle of Germany—but also because of politicians who were reacting in a populistic way to a public—voters!—that was unwilling to come to terms with the past.

To avoid any misunderstandings here, it should be mentioned that the other German state, the GDR, did not face up to the Nazi past either. As we all know, its leadership had, after all, declared itself one of the victors of World War II, and proclaimed all "its" Germans to be anti-fascists: fantastic lies concocted by an "anti-fascism ordained from above" which prevented any real process of appraising Nazism, in spite of the anti-Nazi window dressing which the East German regime had given itself.

Let me summarize: the memories of persecution, which

44

have not only endured but have actually become ever more present in our minds; and the virtually collective exoneration of the perpetrators, the "Grand Peace" that was made with them, the "second guilt"—these are the *two* burdens which weigh down on the survivors of the Holocaust.

So, when all is said and done, is there any room left for a sense of belonging?

But there *must* be something to offset this dual burden! Otherwise, would I not have made off a long time ago, giving in to the urge to escape, an urge that had been so deeply implanted in me by the Nazis? Would I not have done what had been such an obvious option before liberation, indeed as obvious as the fact that the sun would rise the next day—namely, leave Germany, shake its blood-stained dust from my feet forever and bid it farewell, once and for all?

So, the question must be: Why have I stayed in Germany?

5.

If I were to give a simple answer to this question, it might be: I stayed here because my ties to this country were stronger than the damage it had inflicted on me—and the ties must be strong indeed, for the damage, as already mentioned, proved to be irreparable.

But if I wanted to be more precise about it, I would have to say: There was not one, but a whole variety of reasons for my deciding to stay in Germany.

What were they then, what are they now?

I stayed because, as it turned out, it was impossible to leave behind those starving people in a devastated city to whom my family and I owed our lives; people who had helped us, although they knew that their lives would have been worth just as little as our own if the Gestapo had found us in our hiding place. And these people who saved our lives were German.

45

I stayed because it soon became clear that the perpetrators had stayed as well—after they got over the brief shock of retaliation, they were back in operation. Having become aware of the "second guilt" at an early date, I would have felt like a deserter if I had left Germany then—it would have followed me wherever I went.

I have stayed because German is my native language, a creation with which I have never felt the slightest dissonance, not even during the darkest Nazi period, a living creature which lends us a universal ability to express ourselves down to the very last capillaries of the human soul, the wonderful instrument of a writer who could never have written in another language, although his IQ is not underdeveloped.

I have stayed because I feel close to Hamburg, my home town, the setting of my novel, *The Bertinis*—an indissoluble bond, in spite of all that happened there.

I have stayed because, in addition to the powerful "anti-German" feelings within me during the first phase after liberation, I slowly came to realize, though it seems to have taken as long as it does for one Ice Age to replace another, that there are not only individual Germans but many millions of Germans who are my compatriots! And I feel that this is one of the most precious insights of my life.

These Germans who are my compatriots are the breeding ground for a new feeling of belonging that the people in my biography are developing toward in this Germany of the unforgettable primordial experiences. They are the people who believe in the same things I do, and they are everywhere, in every village, in every town and city. Not that they represent the majority, but they are nonetheless a strong force against indifference, organized stultification and malicious insistence. I consider the force a political motor which is insurmountable, at least under the conditions of a democratic republic—and, in terms of historical plausibilities, I see no better alternative to this force for a long time to come.

The day-to-day community of federated Germans, men,

women, young people—*they* are the center of my feeling of belonging.

6.

Even so, it will never be the same as it is for others who have never been ostracized. And I will always feel threatened, threatened by fears which go way back, back to those early years I spoke of in the beginning, but also by contemporary phenomena.

For my sense of belonging naturally comes under heavy attack from that smoldering racist faction which is spreading over united Germany and is far from being stamped out. It is dampened by that notorious, Nazi-inspired misanthropy which lurks behind the guise of xenophobia, which has cost dozens of lives and hundreds, and I mean hundreds, of casualties. But even though I myself am seriously threatened by the anti-democratic right wing, even though I am shattered by the passive stance taken by the government power monopoly towards the danger from the right and am aware of a dismaying lack of courage among citizens to stand up for the victims, I still do not believe that the "ugly Germans" will score another triumph in history.

In one of my most recent books—*Wird Deutschland wieder gefährlich?* (Is Germany Becoming Dangerous Again?)—my answer to the title question was: "Not without trusting in Germany's political, economic and military integration into the European Community and the international commitments this involves; and I am still firmly convinced that the majority of Germans, today and tomorrow, will have enough good common sense not to engage in a new life-and-death confrontation with such a completely different world, not again; and then, for the third time, to try and strike out on a course of its own, which could very well leave Germany once again as the loser. All of this at the end of the 20th century, after careful deliberation and with a view that goes a good bit beyond the threshold of the 21st century, I still sense that I would be more inclined to answer the title question of my book in the negative—with a prudently skeptical optimism."

That was my answer to the basic question as to the future of Europe and the world.

It is strictly at odds with the frequent accusation made of me and my work: "unadulterated Germanophobia . . ."

And I will admit that there are times when I would like to scream "Oh, if only we were!" Those are the times when I feel like running away, giving up, making a decision: Those years between 1933 and 1945 and the 50 years after that—that's enough, more than enough. But—I can't. I am, like Heinrich Heine was, literally nailed to this country, to what is German. It has never asked me what I want or do not want, it holds on to me, hopelessly and with no prospect for change. This is what will not let me go, and it would have followed me everywhere, no matter where I would have gone.

But do not think this is an easy confession for me to make!

I want my problems as a survivor of the Holocaust to be seen and heard, for they are not only mine. I want this Germany to know that in it, even now and most likely into the next century, there are eyewitnesses who cannot forget and do not want to forget. I want it to know that some of them are people who are inevitably reminded of the gas chambers in Auschwitz, or the gas trucks of Chelmno, whenever they have to breathe the exhaust fumes in the traffic jams of our motorized affluent society. People who have to think of Babi Yar, Lidice, Oradour-sur-Glane at the sight of a wound, or a drop of blood. People who tremble whenever the *Lingua tertii imperii*, the language of the Third Reich, of the monsters, is perpetuated in a way which is as inflationary as it is incomprehensible—using the word *"Einsatz"* (commando), for example, heedless of the fact that the mobile death squads, the *Einsatzgruppen* operating behind the German eastern front, caused millions of deaths.

No, my sense of belonging will not be easy, not ever and not for anyone—of that I am sure.

Epilogue

"How on earth can a Jew live in Germany with all of these burdens weighing down on him?"

That is the question I am most often asked, by Jews and non-Jews alike, both here and abroad, and I have been asked it for almost 50 years now.

I have tried to give an answer in these pages.

And behind it is a motto for life that does not come easily for anyone. It must be suffered and fought for, and it guides me like a compass which has never failed me to this very moment, and will continue to show me the way. It is:

"Auschwitz—and life!"

Buchenwald Times Three

by Ernst Cramer

For the first 25 years of my life, Weimar was for me, as it was for nearly all other Germans, simply the town of the wise Duchess Anna Amalia. She had engaged the Swabian poet and scholar Christoph Martin Wieland to tutor her son, later Duke Karl August of Weimar, in her residential palace and thus laid the cornerstone which, only shortly thereafter, prompted the French writer Germaine de Staël to remark that Weimar was the "the capital of belles lettres in Germany."

Goethe, Schiller and Herder, the great masters of 18th century German literature, lived and worked here. It was here that Martin Gropius, together with his friends, established Bauhaus, the cradle of Modernist design. This was where the German National Assembly convened after World War I to draft the constitution which laid the foundations for the first German republic. The enlightened spirit of the great figures of Weimar was to shape the thought, actions and policies of the post-Imperial democratic German Reich. The very term "Weimar Republic" was conceived of as a trendsetting agenda instilled with hope; only later did it come to be misused as a term of abuse by millions of people.

Weimar. Until the fall of 1938, I still considered it the embodiment of the most refined culture, a symbol of the true Germany, so dear to me. Yet, this all changed with a bang—in the truest sense of the words—after the "spontaneous" pogroms organized by the Nazi leadership, the waves of pillaging and lootings of November 9 and 10, 1938. In Weimar, and even more so in the nearby Buchenwald concentration camp, I came to know, indeed I personally experienced, what horrors human beings are capable of inflicting on each other.

Ever since those days, now already more than half a century ago, whenever I hear or read the name Weimar, an icy shudder comes over me as if to remind me of death.

I am well aware of the fact that everything which I myself and thousands of fellow prisoners experienced in Weimar and Buchenwald and which many others went through in Dachau and Sachsenhausen in 1938 was mere child's play compared to the inferno which raged only a few short years later, symbolized by the names Auschwitz, Maidanek and Treblinka. But this knowledge merely makes the chill which runs through my bones at the unextinguishable memories even icier.

Of course, I am being bitterly unfair to the town of Weimar and also to most of its citizens, especially those of subsequent generations. The city, its palaces, churches and villas, the parks, gardens and cemeteries, cannot be held responsible for what subhumans did there between 1938 and 1945—and what others did there at a later date. No more than can any of the younger people, who were still children at the time or were born thereafter. I am glad that they do not have to feel the clammy dread which never ceases to come over me.

This feeling of horror was also present when, as an American soldier at the time, I saw the newly liberated Buchenwald concentration camp again in April 1945. It was even more intense when I returned to Weimar for the first time after the war, some 47 years later. And ever since, the selfsame sense of dread has filled me each time I have gone back there.

It is easy to explain why almost half a century elapsed before I returned to Weimar. During the Soviet occupation, which lasted, albeit in a different form, until the end of 1989, I had never traveled to Communist East Germany or to any other Communist country for that matter (just as I did not visit Spain until after Franco's death). Now, however, the time seemed to have come for me to embark on such a journey into my own past, in spite of many reservations about it.

I arrived in Weimar by express train on a warm July day in 1992. Although so many years had intervened, I was overcome by the past far more strongly than I had imagined. There were only a handful of people there; everything was orderly, quiet and peaceful. But that was not what I felt inside.

The passageway under the train station seemed to be filled with hundreds of frightened, sobbing or screaming people who had been chased down the steps like sheep and beaten against the walls by men in brown-gray uniforms. Men in uniforms also blocked the exits. The victims were being harried by bayonets, rubber truncheons and leather straps.

The memory of November 12, 1938 had come alive. I again heard the moans of those who were in agony and the howling of the SS units at bay. Next to me and in front of me, I saw the victims herded together and also felt the pain of the blows that kept raining down, even through the thick cloth coat my mother had bought for me only a few days before from what she had scrimped and saved. Somehow the coat also managed to cover my friend J., and then a little gray-haired man with a bloody nose who had stumbled on the steps and whom I had simply grabbed by the arm and pulled along with me.

At that time, I was one of about 10,000 German Jews who had been taken into "protective custody" in the aftermath of the pogroms following the attack on the diplomat Ernst vom Rath in Paris, and were being transported to Weimar under armed surveillance and transferred from there to the Buchenwald concentration camp; 20,000 others were sent to Dachau or Sachsenhausen.

On my visit in the summer of 1992, I tore myself away from the stifling images of the past, slowly went out in front of the train station and took a taxi to my hotel.

Things had been different in 1938. After what seemed to me like an eternity—or was it only a few minutes?—a whistle blew. We were then drubbed toward the exit.

There were any number of trucks standing out in front of the train station. At a brisk trot, much too fast for some older people, we were forced onto them; SS men grabbed hold of a few of the feeble by their hands and feet and simply threw them onto the back of the trucks, which were already over-filled. Then the cars were hermetically sealed with canvas. The drive into uncertainty began.

Now, a half a century later, I wanted to see what was still left of the Buchenwald camp. I soon drove to the area on the Ettersberg. This was where the Nazis had set up their third concentration camp in 1937. Initially it had been called "Camp Ettersberg." But the "Nazi Culture Society of Weimar" had protested, saying that the name Ettersberg was associated with Goethe. In fact, author Ernst Wiechert, an inmate of Buchenwald, later wrote about the oak tree between the laundry and the kitchen, under which "Goethe and Charlotte von Stein had already sat."

I knew the street leading to the former camp. Not from November 1938; we had not been able to get a glimpse outside from where we were in the darkened truck until it stopped right in front of the gate and we were again herded through the puddles and over piles of gravel amidst blows and scorn. But I had, after all, been there in the meantime.

In spring 1945, during the final weeks of the war, I was quartered with my American unit for several days in a brickworks near Eisenach. (Thanks to a U.S. visa, I had been able to make it to safety in the summer of 1939 after my release from Buchenwald. I had voluntarily signed up for the U.S. Army the day after the attack on Pearl Harbor, when the United States also entered the war against Nazi Germany.)

On April 14, 1945 I drove to Buchenwald with my commanding officer to question prisoners there. American units had occupied the camp the day before, which the SS guard units had deserted shortly before that.

On the cul-de-sac which led to the camp, emaciated figures ran, or rather tumbled, towards us. They begged us for food and cigarettes. Others were lying dead at the side of the road.

In the camp itself, we were met with horrifying scenes. Doctors and medics were trying to save the lives of some who were at death's door. Many ex-prisoners just kept lying there in the barracks, too weak to get up. Corpses were still scattered here and there. Other bodies had been stacked like deadwood on box carts.

This brief stay in April 1945 was a dreadful experience, even worse than the weeks in the fall of 1938, when I myself had been a prisoner. What already seemed like hell to us then had in the meantime become a nightmare of the damned.

When I returned more than forty years later, an almost eery calm hung over the site. None of the wooden huts were still standing. Only a few of the stone structures have been preserved—the commander's headquarters, for example, or the building that housed the political department, and the shed that was used for clothing and equipment. In the flat, open area, the former huts, called blocks, are outlined on the stony ground.

A few visitors go from one set of markings to the next, to the Polish camp, for example, where 126 prisoners were left to starve in a barbed-wire cage after the war started; or to the detention cell, the notorious "bunker," where people were tortured or slaughtered from the outset. During my time in the camp, Pastor Paul Schneider, a courageous man, was locked up there in solitary confinement, but he never stopped shouting out of his cell window that he believed in God and justice; he was eventually murdered.

All of the things which happened here half a century ago are so hard for visitors to imagine today that they often cannot quite conjure up what life was like back then, in spite of all the labels, signs and photographs. They move swiftly from one point to the next, somewhat at a loss.

It was different for me, of course. Out on the yard where we had to line up for roll call, I looked for the spot where I

54

had to do 100 knee-bends one morning; and also the spot where an epileptic from Marburg was stomped to death after he had a seizure; and also the spot where an SS man hit me over my closely shaven head about 20 times with a wooden board: On the third morning or so after arriving in the concentration camp, I had volunteered for a special detachment, not yet knowing that the worst thing you could do in a camp was to draw attention to yourself in some way or other. There were 12 of us young men who had to carry the sick and the dead out of the five wooden huts to which we were assigned and take them over to the laundry, which served as a field hospital and mortuary.

Meanwhile, everyone else had to stand at attention for roll call in blocks of hundreds, which had been grouped according to height.

When we were through with our macabre job, we were assigned to the block with the hundred shortest people—all 12 of us were a good eight inches taller than our neighbors. An SS man in an immaculate black uniform tried to eliminate this lack of symmetry by hitting each of us over the head with a wooden board. Fortunately, the loudspeaker snarled the order "All Jew-birds, go straight to your huts!" before the blows could do any more damage to our skulls than a few bumps and bruises. In the summer of 1992, it was as if I could still feel the pounding in my head.

I saw, I even smelled the people who had stood next to me. I heard their moans as well as the shrill voices of the guards shouting some order or other from the gate.

Then I went to the spot, slightly off the beaten path, where the "little camp" had been set up in the fall of 1938, separated from the rest of the area by a fence. Five wooden huts had been put up in great haste especially for the prisoners of November 1938. The huts had no doors or windows, just an open aisle down the middle leading off to both sides.

The bunks consisted of five levels of wooden planks with about 2 feet of space between them. There were no blankets, wash basins or latrines. Heaps of lime were meant to blot out the stench and prevent epidemics.

These "blocks" were torn down after the special "Jewish campaign" was over in February 1940.

I myself was released after six weeks. My name was called one morning, and then things went pretty fast. I was shaved again and then forced to sign a statement saying that I, like all other prisoners, had been well-treated and would leave Germany within a stipulated period of time.

The very next morning, five other prisoners and I were put on a train which had been stopped in a makeshift station near the camp. It was a passenger train bound for Halle and from there for Jena. They pushed us into a compartment that was full of smoking, chattering laborers who were on their way to work. When we got on, everyone fell so silent you could hear a pin drop. The men stood up and offered us their seats. They could tell from our shaven heads, our hollow cheeks and our dirty clothes where we were coming from.

"From the concentration camp?" one asked. "Shut up," another said, interrupting him abruptly. Nothing more was said after that.

However, later, when we changed trains in Halle, three of us found sandwiches in our coat-pockets, and I found a shiny Reichsmark as well. The workers had slipped them into our pockets.

At the train station in Breslau, I went to the men's toilet. A big, stout lavatory attendant came up to me and asked in a raucous voice: "You Jewish?" I nodded and was afraid she would tell me to get out; maybe this place was supposed to be kept "free of Jews" as well. But that was not the case, because she said just as loudly as before: "Then you can use this for nothing today" and unlocked one of the stalls for me.

So, they are not all beasts, that became clear to me then. As Abraham said in his dialogue with the Lord over the fate of Sodom and Gomorrah, there are always some "righteous" people in every situation.

They are not all beasts. But of course they are not all angels either, I would hasten to add.

Now that there are groups in postwar Germany who again want to substitute the use of violence for legitimate political struggle, my memory has gone into overdrive. Whatever the motives may be: whenever left-wing roughnecks get into street fights with right-wing hooligans, I am reminded of similar scenes from the final years of the Weimar Republic. No matter how much those groups fought each other back then, they were unanimous in their rejection of democracy and its institutions. Indeed, groups of right-wing and left-wing extremists joined forces more than once and took to the streets, rabble-rousing and murdering, united in their hatred of the "decadent system," of the state order.

The escalation of nationalistic and racist attacks since the days of the bloodless revolution for reunification in 1989, a trend which has not been restricted to the new east German states, has led to comparisons being made (not only in this country but also abroad) with the way things were before. They are analogies with those vicious attacks which were the harbingers of disaster more than six decades ago, and which paved the way for the times of German self-degradation during the Nazi period. Like then, the extremist right-wing rabble-rousers are there, side by side with their extremist left-wing counterparts. There are those who have a feeling of déjà vu.

The damage that was done by excessive nationalism a half a century ago seems to have been forgotten—much as many today already want to repress what 40 years of Communism in Germany did to the people and the country. It is indeed creepy when skinheads scream *"Sieg Heil"* on the site of Buchenwald and demonstrate with their arms raised in the Hitler salute; when they dig out the old Nazi symbols for themselves; and when they desecrate graves, especially the graves of Jews. And the murders committed against foreigners by right-wing extremists are just as disgraceful as the attacks committed by leftist fanatics against the captains of finance and industry such as (former Deutsche Bank chairman) Alfred Herrhausen and (the erstwhile head of Treuhand, the German agency in charge of privatization) Detlev Karsten Rohwedder.

What is even worse is that there are far too many who, while not condoning the attacks, nonetheless sympathize with the motives. One must have some understanding for the fact, so they argue, that young people want to defend themselves against foreigners who take their jobs, their apartments and their girlfriends away from them; that young, unemployed Germans are defending themselves against "black-market Vietnamese" or "conniving gypsy thieves." In much the same way some people "secretly" applauded when other, much more intelligent young left-wing fanatics went on a murderous hunt for "representatives of capitalism."

Déjà vu—is all of this the prelude to a repetition of the events which took place in the 1930s and 1940s? The answer is definitely "No."

Unlike the situation during the Weimar period, democracy is so firmly anchored in Germany today that it can hardly be jeopardized by fringe groups, no matter how loud and distasteful they may be. Extremists may even be elected to parliament from time to time. But they will never have a decisive influence on politics.

The icy shudder that will never leave me admonishes me to remember the past. But I am confident in the future.

And I am also convinced that Weimar can again become a capital of belles lettres for the younger generation, as I think of Goethe's verse:

"O Weimar! dir fiel ein besonder Los!
Wie Bethlehem in Juda, klein und groß.
Bald wegen Geist und Witz beruft dich weit
Europens Mund, bald wegen Albernheit.
Der stille Weise schaut und sieht geschwind
Wie zwei Extreme nah verschwistert sind."

58

(Oh Weimar! to you has fallen a special fate!
Like Bethlehem in Judah, small and great.
For intellect and wit shall your name be known
in all of Europe, and for stupidity alone.
The quiet wiseman sees and swiftly contemplates
how closely the two extremes relate.)

The 50th anniversary of the liberation will soon be celebrated in Buchenwald. I will go back to Weimar and be there, in spite of the Furies of Remembrance who have never left me since my first stay on the Ettersberg.

Notes and Reflections
on Jews in Germany

by Ignatz Bubis

The history of the Jews in Germany began as far back as the year 331, when the Jewish community in Cologne was first founded. Over the ensuing period of more than 1,600 years, Jews have continually lived in Germany, under widely differing conditions and, for centuries, in medieval ghettos.

In 1812, the decree of the Prussian king heralded the age of equal civil rights for Jews in Germany, a trend that was intensified after the revolution of 1848 and culminated in full equal rights around 1870. It was at this time that so-called German Jewry came into being. Many of the Jews living in Germany considered the country to be the promised land of the future, one which could serve as a substitute for Palestine. Needless to say, around the turn of the century a Zionist movement emerged in Germany as well, but it only gained momentum after World War I. Emigration to Palestine on a notable scale did not occur, however, until the early 1930s. At this time, roughly 600,000 Jews were living in Germany, excluding assimilated Jews who, for whatever reason, did not wish to be members of the Jewish community.

German Jewry as it then existed disappeared with the Shoah*, or rather was destroyed by it. Approximately 400,000 Jews managed to flee the Nazis in time; of the remainder, approximately 170,000 were murdered during the Nazi era. Only 12,000 of these German Jews survived the Nazis, be it by hiding illegally or by being hidden by friends, or as survivors of the death camps. Of this figure, several thousand decided to emigrate after 1945, while a few thousand of those who had emigrated in time then returned to Germany.

★★★

The Jewish Community in Germany today has some 43,000 members, and there are between 5,000 and 10,000 citizens who are members of the Jewish faith but who have elected not to become members of the community. The community as a whole consists of 76 individual communities. Half of the total membership is concentrated in three major cities: 10,000 members live in Berlin, over 6,000 in Frankfurt/Main and over 5,000 in Munich. If we take three other large cities into account, namely Cologne, Düsseldorf and Hamburg, then this covers almost 70 percent of the overall membership. In other words, only about 13,000 Jews live in the 70 other communities, including those in eastern Germany.

This German Jewish community has very little in common with the Jewish communities as they existed in Germany prior to 1933.

After the end of World War II and the tragic consequences it had had for European Jewry, hardly anyone believed that Jewish life could re-emerge in Germany.

In those days, the Jewish Restitution Successor Organization and the Claims Conference saw themselves as handling indemnification for the German Jewish communities. From 1945 until 1950, approximately 250,000 to 300,000 Jewish survivors came to Germany, but not in order to stay. They were instead classified as Displaced Persons and lived in camps until they could emigrate to what was then Palestine, to Australia, Canada, the United States, and other countries. Ninety percent of these Jews did indeed emigrate and the remainder sat on packed suitcases waiting to leave. Quite a few years went by before many of the packed suitcases were unpacked again.

From 1950 to 1989, between 26,000 and 30,000 Jews were living in the two Germanies, although only 400 of them were residents of East Germany. By no means all of the Jews living in West Germany were German citizens.

To date, the fluctuation in the Jewish population has generally been above the average for Germany as a whole. New immigrants come to Germany from eastern European countries, and new emigrants leave, heading in particular for Israel or the United States.

Many of those who remained in Germany and particularly the two postwar generations born in the country chose to become naturalized, so that the number of German citizens of Jewish faith steadily increased up to 1989 and formed the majority of the Jewish community. This picture has changed in the last five years insofar as about 14,000 Jews from the former Soviet Union have immigrated to Germany, so that a large number of the Jews living here now do not possess German citizenship.

One way or another, Jewish life in Germany has gone through more changes than that of other religious minorities.

An entirely new "Jewish infrastructure" was established in postwar Germany. In the meantime, there are several Jewish primary schools, a Jewish high school in Berlin, kindergartens, adult education programs and Jewish homes for senior citizens, not to mention the synagogues.

The Jewish communities in Germany are united bodies, even if there is a pluralism of thought within the community. Regardless of whether members considers themselves to be Reform Jews, liberal or Orthodox Jews, they are all members of the same community. This is understandable given the small number of Jews living in Germany. Thus, within the individual communities there are occasionally Reform and liberal rabbis. However, most of the 12 rabbis in Germany consider themselves members of Orthodox Jewry.

★★★

German unification has had no impact on the Jewish communities in Germany.

At first, it was widely believed that the dissolution of the former German Democratic Republic (East Germany) and its incorporation into the Federal Republic of Germany (West Germany) had intensified anti-Semitism and that negative attitudes towards the Jews were coming primarily from the new federal states in the east. However, this is not the case. Anti-Semitism has never ceased to exist in Germany, but it has not become stronger in recent years. Certainly, the anti-Semitism of the 1930s and 1940s, which was aimed at the destruction of Judaism, no longer exists. However, this is not to say that anti-Semitism has been stamped out; it is very much alive, both latently and, in part, quite manifestly. Things have changed solely to the extent that until a few years ago, anti-Semites did not openly profess their anti-Semitism, whereas today, many have no qualms about admitting their prejudices.

The desecration of Jewish cemeteries or monuments is no longer a rare occurrence and the number of such acts is now higher than it was in the 1930s. It is often adolescents or even school children who perpetrate these crimes; they know little or nothing about Nazi ideology and yet they are often inspired to commit such deeds because they have blindly accepted xenophobic and anti-Semitic slogans. It is also true that there are still diehard Nazis and neo-Nazis in the population, but the number is relatively small.

The number of members and followers of the extreme right-wing parties is lower in Germany than in neighboring countries and it would appear to be on the decline.

By contrast, the incidence of acts of violence has increased markedly and 90 percent of such acts are carried out by young people. While the total number of violent activists is admittedly not high, the damage they cause is enormous and greater than in neighboring countries. Yet it is also worthy of mention that, seen overall, the younger generation is less xenophobic or anti-Semitic than the older generation.

What has increased in recent years in Germany is xenophobia. This has frequently and erroneously been equated with animosity toward non-Germans. Clear differentiation is in order here, for this xenophobia is not directed toward the French, the English, the Dutch, the Danish or white Americans, for instance, but above all toward Sinti and Romani people, black Africans, Turks—in other words, against all those people who are visibly foreign or "alien." Citizenship plays no role here. Such xenophobia is directed just as much against Sinti and Romani people or Turks who are German citizens as it is against Jews, who are regarded by the majority of German society as foreigners. Here, we have a remnant from the ideology of the 1930s and 1940s, which caused Jews to be ostracized for belonging to a different race.

★★★

It has been the events of recent years which led me to entitle the book containing a part-biography of my life: *I Am a German Citizen of the Jewish Faith*.

After World War I, my parents came to Germany from Russia (or rather the Soviet Union), and from Germany we went to Poland in 1935.

My mother came from Russian Poland and my maternal grandparents lived in Poland.

Following the German invasion of Poland in 1939, I found myself in February 1941 in the ghetto of Deblin, which was the city we had lived in since 1935. In the fall of 1942, after the deportations and the liquidation of the ghetto, I fled to a slave labor camp.

During the deportations, my father was sent to Treblinka, where he was murdered; my mother had already died in December 1940. At that time I still had a sister and a brother, whereas my four other siblings had either died as infants or adolescents.

Following Hitler's invasion of the Soviet Union, both my sister and my brother were murdered by the Nazis after having fled in 1939 to the part of Poland occupied by the Soviets.

64

I remained in the Deblin slave labor camp until June 1944 and was then sent to a labor camp near Czestochova, where I was liberated by Soviet troops in January 1945. In the late summer of 1945, I returned again to Wroclaw (Breslau), but did not wish to stay there. As early as November 1945 I traveled via Dresden to West Berlin. As of 1949, I lived first in Stuttgart, then in Pforzheim and, from November 1956 onwards, in Frankfurt.

When I returned to Germany in 1945, I did not intend to stay there. I, too, sat on packed suitcases. In the course of the years, however, I grew to have confidence in German democracy, and it must have been in 1956, although I was not aware of it at the time, that I finally decided to remain in Germany.

***

The Federal Republic of Germany was founded in 1949 and endowed with an exemplary constitution (although it is regrettable that Article 16 on the fundamental right to asylum was substantially altered in 1993). Over the years, the country has proved itself to be a sound democracy. This was not changed by the incorporation of East Germany in 1989. German unification dissolved an undemocratic Stalinistic sub-state and integrated it into democratic Germany. Whereas in the early 1930s, the majority of the citizens of the Reich voted for extremist parties, since the inception of the Federal Republic, a steady 90 percent of the electorate have voted for democratic parties.

Although there has been a noticeable slight shift to the right in all of the democratic parties in recent times, I do not believe that this threatens democracy in Germany in any way. The democratic parties believe that Germany's future lies within the European Union. There is a consensus that the European Union must be strengthened and advanced; this commitment has been in no way weakened by German unification.

The democratic parties are fully conscious of the responsibility that has devolved to them as a result of Nazi history, and they have also accepted their share of the responsibility for that era. Recently, however, there have been signs that a minority of the population would like to confine the Nazi era to the history books and allow it to be forgotten. This must never happen. The Jewish community considers itself responsible for preserving the memory, purely for the sake of the present and future, *to ensure that history does not repeat itself.*

Never Forget Thy People Israel! Autobiographical Remarks

by Julius H. Schoeps

Our identity and consciousness is always defined by our origins and place of birth. I am no exception. I was born in 1942, in Stockholm, where my parents met in emigrant circles. From what both of them told me, I know that their flight had been highly risky and that they had found it very hard to gain a foothold in their new surroundings. My mother worked as a domestic, while my father was able to pursue his academic studies in the libraries and archives with a stipend from the church. My mother's income and my father's scholarship were just barely sufficient for them to live on.

After I was born, I lived with my parents at first, but they eventually put me into the care of foster parents. This was because the refugees in Sweden feared an invasion by the Wehrmacht. My parents thought that, if worst came to worst, it would be safer for their child to be out in the country. I later learned that several hundred Jewish children had been hidden by Swedish farmers. After the war, there were tragic incidents. Many of these farmers refused to give up the children whom they had taken in.

Roots in German Judaism

On my father's side, I come from a German-Jewish family with roots in the Altmark (Brandenburg) and in West Prussia. The Schoeps family had lived in the little town of Neuenburg between Graudenz and Marienwerder since the middle of the 18th century. According to one story that runs in the family, the name goes back to the legendary Kabbalistic messiah Shabbetai Tzevi (1626–1676), whose disciples were called "Schapse" or "Schepse." I still like the idea that my forefathers supposedly followed a false messiah. Why not? But is it really true? I have my doubts. All we know is that the Schoepses were firmly rooted people, usually small shopkeepers, who often owned a piece of farmland.

My grandfather, after whom I was named, was the first to climb the social ladder. He was a general practitioner on Hasenheide, a major thoroughfare in Berlin, where he worked as a family doctor for 47 years, until the Nazis took his medical license away. My grandfather was the only Jew in the Empress Alexandra of Russia Second Guard Dragoon Regiment and he was proud of having achieved the rank of major in the medical corps of the reserves. Not too long ago, a Bundeswehr barracks in Hildesheim was named after him.

My mother's side of the family also comes from Prussia. Moses Mendelssohn, the great "German Socrates," as he was admiringly called by his contemporaries, was one of my ancestors. But there is also a line of descent leading to David Friedländer, Mendelssohn's pupil, who in a conversation with Provost Teller is known to have made an offer of a modified conversion to Christianity on the part of the Jews.

The Jews, Friedländer said in his famous *Missive*, would make certain concessions on their ritual laws and the Christians would give up Christology (as we know, Schleiermacher positively derided the efforts of enlightened Jewish circles to propagate a form of "Christianity without Christ"). To this day, I am still fascinated by Friedländer's ecumenical idea, although I realize, of course, that a construct of this kind, in which the concept of religion is based on Enlightenment and rationality, is bound to fail—human beings would always get in their own way.

My father, who even as a young man had a passion for the

philosophy of religion and Jewish theology, would most likely not have shared my interest in Friedländer. He was a supporter of Salomon Ludwig Steinheim, whose doctrine of revelation fascinated him. Steinheim, a somewhat unconventional 19th century philosopher, had attempted in his own variation on Kantian positions to formulate a Jewish theology that would transcend liberalism and Orthodoxy. His position was more or less comparable to that of Kierkegaard in Christianity. In 1985, when we were looking for a name to give our newly founded institute for German-Jewish history, we decided on the name of this religious philosopher, physician and poet, who has for the most part been forgotten today. I shall return to this later.

I still admire my father today for not having told his two sons how to think or what to believe. He was of the opinion that we should make up our own minds. The most enduring impression was made by a letter from my father, which he wrote when I was six months old. It was written in the style of Matthias Claudius and appealed to his son never to forget his Jewish origins: "Never forget thy people Israel!" The letter, which was presented to me 13 years later for my bar mitzvah, went on to say, among other things: "I do not want to make any rules for you . . . The same applies to religious life and religious convictions. In such matters in particular I condemn any form of coercion . . ."

After my brother and I returned to postwar Germany, where we joined my father, the latter attempted to bring us closer to the religious traditions and customs of Judaism. At first we held Shabbos on Friday evenings at home, and on the High Holidays we drove to the Community in Nuremberg. At that time, the Community did not yet have a proper synagogue of its own. Like nearly all synagogues in Germany, the old one had been destroyed by the Nazis in 1938. After the end of the war, the Community and its administration were provisionally housed in a nondescript apartment building in Wielandstrasse. I still have a clear picture of the way from the bus station to Friedrich Ebert Platz. A few steps toward the center of town, then a right into Wielandstrasse, the second or third house down. A garden in the front, then the entrance to the meetinghouse.

In those days, we were living in a non-Jewish world. There were no Jewish children our age for my brother and me to play with. The people we met were older, usually concentration camp survivors. As far as I can remember, I never heard anyone laugh. I can still remember one of them as if it were only yesterday. An elderly man, with snow-white hair. He used to be a master clockmaker. We only knew him as Herr Auerbach. I cannot remember his first name, if I ever knew it at all. It is said that he survived by hiding in Nuremberg. After all he had been through, it was probably a kind of mitzvah, or a good deed, for him to give me and my brother instruction in Hebrew and prepare us for the bar mitzvah. I can still see his calloused hands in front of me. He ran his index finger, word by word, through the Hebrew prayer texts which my brother and I were supposed to decipher. It was very hard for us.

Life Among the Non-Jews

As a 12 or 13 year-old, I was probably unable to understand why I should have religious instruction in Judaism. After all, I was living in a non-Jewish world for the most part. So why learn Hebrew? Why read prayer texts that I didn't understand? If someone had asked me at the time whether my Jewishness meant anything to me, I would presumably not have been able to give a satisfactory answer.

At that time, I was sent to boarding school because of my poor performance in school. I went to Obersalzberg near Berchtesgaden, where I spent a few years sharing a classroom with children of former Nazi bigwigs. This was not a problem for me back then. Years later, however, when I met a few of my former schoolmates again, it was harder for me. We—both they and I—sensed that something had come between us. It was almost impossible to carry on a conversation any longer, the days of naive spontaneity were clearly over.

The postwar years were marked by a halcyon calm. Hardly anyone talked about the time under Hitler, let alone German-Jewish relations. Reconstruction consumed all of our energy and blocked out of our minds everything that had anything to do with the period between 1933 and 1945. Only occasional allusions were made to it at home. Ella Friedemann, my father's aunt, who moved in with us in Erlangen, never said anything. She did not want to talk about her experiences. Many years later I found out that she and her daughter Susi had survived because other people had helped them hide.

In his book of memoirs entitled *Die letzten dreissig Jahre und danach* (The last 30 years and thereafter), which was published in 1956, my father confessed that it weighed on his soul that hundreds of thousands of people were killed and he had not warned them in time to flee at all costs. He read me the book, chapter by chapter, in his study. At the time, I did not yet understand the tragedy behind his remark that he had stood up for the Germanness of the German Jews.

My father suffered a great deal for having supported a cause which was no longer understood in postwar Germany. When a Berlin newspaper publisher with a dubious past accused him in the late 1960s of having collaborated with the Nazis, something collapsed inside him. He had growing doubts about whether he had done the right thing in coming out of Swedish exile and returning to Germany. "Malice," he once told me with a bitter undertone in his voice, "must be part of the German national character."

But let us return to my own story. After finishing secondary school, I began my studies at Friedrich Alexander University in Erlangen in the early 1960s. I was only marginally interested in problems of Judaism at the time. I enrolled in seminars and lecture courses in theater studies, journalism, history and liberal arts, and I was thinking about pursuing a career somewhere between theater arts and book editing.

When I transferred from Erlangen to Berlin, I started to become more interested in historical issues. However, I was bored by the courses offered at the Friedrich Meinecke Institute at the Free University of Berlin because of their conventional format and their traditional approach. The seminars offered by Adolf Leschnitzer, who was living like a recluse there as an honorary professor, were an exception. Few people strayed into his courses, a circumstance I found quite pleasant.

Leschnitzer in a sense personified the pre-1933 German-Jewish symbiosis, the existence of which Gershom Scholem was just beginning to dispute at that time. But Scholem was not yet the guru he became in the 1960s and '70s on the wave of the Walther Benjamin revival. I was not yet familiar with Scholem's verdict at that time and perhaps that was why I could sit so happily in Leschnitzer's seminars and ponder the problems involved in the history of German-Jewish relations, which were beginning to interest me more and more.

I was attracted by the student movement of the 1960s but not to the point of being "in solidarity" with it, as the expression went at the time. Instinctively, I felt that something was being negotiated at the demonstrations and sit-ins which was not my concern. Today I know that the protests of the generation that took to the streets during the late 1960s were unconsciously directed against the Nazi past of their fathers. The protests were directed against the wall of silence with which postwar Germany hermetically sealed itself off from the crimes of the Nazi period.

My critical distance from the student protest movement was intensified when the Left sided with the Palestinians. It annoyed me very much that no distinction was made between anti-Semitism and anti-Zionism—and I began to sense that there was not such a big difference between the anti-Semitism of the fathers and the anti-Zionism of the sons. I can still very well remember one event at the Free University of Berlin which was addressed by the poet Erich Fried. I made an appeal for some understanding of the Zionist positions, with the result that the students, under the spell of Erich Fried, expelled me from the lecture hall amidst a frenzied roar of applause. The rhythmic clapping and chanting still rings in my ears: "*Zionisten raus, Zionisten raus . . .*" (Zionists out!)

Yet, I never became a Zionist in the sense that I made it part of my ambition to emigrate to Israel. I have always defended the existence, and the right to exist, of the State of Israel, but this did not keep me from occasionally criticizing Israeli government policy. In 1982, for example, together with a number of younger Jews I signed a declaration condemning the invasion of Lebanon by the Israeli army. Today I regard the political development of recent years, which has led to a rapprochement between Israelis and Palestinians, as a vindication of the critical position I took at the time.

Signing the declaration cost me my seat on the council of the Düsseldorf Jewish Community. My colleagues on this council did not accept the view which I tried to convey to them, namely that morality, as we know, is indivisible and cannot be readjusted to suit the present moment. When I pointed out that they criticized neo-Nazi attacks but had nothing to say about the crimes in Lebanon, my comment was dismissed in no uncertain terms. Either they did not understand what I was trying to say or they did not want to understand.

Life as a University Professor

Ever since my days as a university student, I have wondered why the Germans were not able to overcome their prejudices and let Jews be Jews. Why, I always asked myself, was the overwhelming majority of the Christian-German environment against the Jews? And why did the Jews, who were well aware of this hostility, strive nonetheless to achieve emancipation and acculturation?

Later, after I had completed my studies and doctoral thesis and went on to address these issues as a professional historian, I soon found out that they were really only questions to myself. I was only partially successful in making the students and colleagues more aware of the German-Jewish problem. If I talked about the fact that German-Jewish history is an integral part of German history, for example, they would nod their heads, but it was clear that they were not all that interested. Only in rare, exceptional cases was I able to overcome this distanced response.

In over 20 years as a professor of political science at Duisburg University, I never managed to get the topics that were of interest to me established as a permanent part of the curriculum. A certain amount of resistance always had to be overcome, because my colleagues could never quite understand what German-Jewish intellectual history had to do with the discipline of political science. They were just about able to accept the inclusion of problems covered by research into anti-Semitism because they thought this might have something to do with the phenomenon of right-wing extremism and could therefore be categorized under the subject heading "domestic policy issues." But they had problems classifying courses which dealt with the ideas of Moses Mendelssohn, Martin Buber or Franz Rosenzweig, for example. Generally speaking, these names meant nothing to most of them.

In the early 1970s, together with two colleagues, I set up a research program devoted to the "History and Religion of Judaism," which paved the way for many research projects, but was especially worthwhile in the revision of school textbooks. The studies submitted to Duisburg on the image of Jews in German history textbooks broke new ground and triggered a number of activities in educational policy, including the German-Israeli textbook conferences, whose recommendations have been incorporated into the subsequent production of textbooks.

The research program eventually spawned the Salomon

Ludwig Steinheim Institute for German-Jewish History, which was founded in 1986. As an interdisciplinary research facility working independently from the university, the Institute focuses on issues connected with the history of German-Jewish relations from the Age of Enlightenment to the present. During the six years of my chairmanship, the Institute not only earned an international reputation but also obtained funding from government sources. One probable reason why we were given this support was that we tried to look at German-Jewish history from an angle that was not restricted exclusively to Auschwitz. In the meantime, our approach, which seeks to understand German-Jewish history as an integral part of German history, has gained widespread acceptance in the academic world.

My own attempts to establish a Jewish Studies program in Duisburg, however, met with considerable resistance. It took a long time before I understood why my colleagues were stonewalling all activities in this direction. In committees where I had to justify the request for a degree program to be established in this area, I was told that, apart from necessitating the creation of new posts, a project of this kind would cost money; money that would be better invested elsewhere. It was hard to overlook a mildly anti-Semitic undertone in some of these statements. It was not until a few years after I had left Duisburg that the idea of a Jewish Studies program was back on the agenda, not out of any interest on the university's part, but because of political pressure; a directive was received from the North Rhine-Westphalian Ministry of Education calling for the course of studies to be introduced.

The Herzl Edition

Preparations for the seven-volume edition of the "Letters and Diaries of Theodor Herzl" also got underway in the late 1970s. Some 15 years on, this project is now nearing completion. The work was made possible with a grant provided by the German Research Society (Deutsche Forschungsgesellschaft—DFG).

Unfortunately, the Herzl edition got embroiled in the "historians' debate,★" which in the late 1980s made a lot of waves on the intellectual scene. When the original Herzl project administrator resigned and Ernst Nolte★ took his place, the editors and staff said they would go along with this appointment only if Nolte's role were limited to managing the funds in the project budget and if he kept his extreme political opinions to himself. However, when Nolte's (in)famous article on "The passage of time" appeared in the *Frankfurter Allgemeine Zeitung*★ on June 6, 1986, equating Auschwitz with the Gulag Archipelago, there was no longer any room for compromise.

The editors and staff of the Herzl edition issued a joint statement declaring that they could not work with a person who relativized the importance of what was the most enormous crime committed by any state in this century. Under the mounting pressure of international protests, the DFG had no choice but to entrust the project administration to someone else. It took a certain amount of chutzpah on the part of Nolte and his followers to cite this case in an attempt, again carried in the *Frankfurter Allgemeine Zeitung*, to show that in Germany the principles of academic freedom were being jeopardized.

Aside from problems of this nature, there was never any doubt that work on the edition would continue. Nor, for political reasons, could anyone have justified breaking it off. Herzl undeniably ranks among the great figures in world history. Indeed, it would have been an irony of world history had the "historians' debate" put an end to the work on the edition. I remember thinking, poor Herzl, you really did not deserve this. If he had been around to see Nolte's attempt to play down the Nazi atrocities, he would have presumably regarded it as a late vindication of his Zionist convictions.

New Beginnings in Potsdam

After the two Germanies were unified in 1990, I moved from North Rhine-Westphalia to the newly created state of Brandenburg. The minister for science and research there had asked whether I might not want to work on establishing a new university in Potsdam with a profile of its own. It did not take me long to decide. For one thing, I welcomed the challenge and, for another, the minister made the tempting suggestion that, in addition to assuming the chair for German-Jewish history, I might like to found something similar to Duisburg's Steinheim Institute in Potsdam. We were both of the opinion that this institute should be European in orientation.

Despite a certain amount of antagonism on the part of some faculty members, it was possible within a relatively short time not only to set up the History Department in Potsdam, but also to establish the Moses Mendelssohn Center for European-Jewish Studies. The staff and I benefitted from the know-how that had been acquired while establishing the Steinheim Institute in Duisburg. I deliberately chose to name the research center after the philosopher Moses Mendelssohn, who not only stands for the family traditions that were cut short by the Nazis but also, in a programmatic sense, for everything to which I had been committed up to that time—enlightenment, justice and tolerance.

When the center was officially opened on June 1, 1994, in the presence of Manfred Stolpe, head of the Brandenburg state government, and many members of his cabinet, it was officially announced that a degree program for Jewish Studies would be established at the University of Potsdam. The design for this course of studies, which the newly installed colleagues and staff of the Mendelssohn Center had developed within a very short period of time, is not like any other in Germany. It is comparable to the Jewish Studies programs in the United States and Israel and, in terms of the wide variety of subjects covered and methods used, it will probably come to take the place of "Judaistics," which at German universities has traditionally centered on philology.

Why I Have Stayed

In conclusion, I shall do my best to answer the question as to why I have opted to stay in Germany. There have been plenty of reasons to leave the country. I am thinking of the recurring desecrations of Jewish cemeteries, of the anti-Semitic statements by some politicians who are considered respectable, or of court rulings which convey a sense of sympathy for xenophobia and the behavior of right-wing extremists. This is highly aggravating for many people. Yet, as unsettling as all of this may be at times, I have never been inclined to dramatize occurrences of this nature. Fortunately.

I had good reasons for staying in Germany which are ultimately personal in nature: a woman with whom I have been living together happily for over 20 years now. Friends I would not want to give up. And a profession that I find fulfilling. If I had become a doctor or an engineer, I might, when I was younger, have considered going away, since doctors and engineers are needed everywhere. But for an historian who, moreover, is concerned with problems of the German-Jewish history of consciousness? It is an advantage for such a person to be living in Germany. He must feel at home in the German language and culture if he wants to appreciate fully the history of German-Jewish relations, with all its high points and its abysmal depths.

Everyone who decides to stay in Germany is almost automatically faced with the question of what this means for one's own identity. At times I ask myself, for example, whether I am a "German citizen of Jewish faith," as it was called before 1933. Or am I someone who is called a German because, given the cultural environment in which I grew up, no other label would be appropriate? The first interpretation is supported by the fact that I hold a German passport, whereas the second is supported by the fact that I grew up in postwar Germany and attended the same schools and universities as most of the people in my generation. I read the same German classics as they did, grappled with Fichte, Hegel and Marx as they did, and was shaped by the general mood that accompanied life in pre-unification West Germany.

The problem of self-definition affects not only my own generation—it was a lifelong source of worry to my father, too. Those who knew him still recall how he always tried to avoid referring to himself as a "German." If someone asked him to define himself, then he usually made use of the formula "Prussian, conservative, Jew." I do not have this option. Although I am a Jew by birth and a conservative in my view of the world—but only in certain respects—I cannot be Prussian because there is no longer any state by that name with which one could identify.

All that remains is for me to conceive of myself as that which I have presumably actually become as a result of my background, education and socialization in postwar Germany: a citizen of the Federal Republic of Germany who has a Jewish identity, but who has been shaped to a great degree by a Protestant environment, who feels and thinks as a German does. In Israel, this type of Jew is called a "yekke:" someone who comes from Germany and is immediately recognizable from the way he looks. Because he is stiff and single-minded, the "yekke" is usually regarded as a pathetic, ridiculous figure. To this day, I have a certain liking for this type, probably because it reminds me of myself.

From time to time, I think about what it is that actually makes me different from the average German. If anything, then I suppose it is mainly the awareness, or rather the feeling, of having had different kinds of experiences and memories. The view of the Nazi regime is a good example of what I mean. It is safe to assume that the period from 1933 to 1945 does not mean very much to the majority of Germans anymore. For them, Nazi Germany and its crimes are mere history now, a distant recollection, which does not bother them or unsettle them in any way. Alexander and Margarete Mitscherlich found an expression for this, which has since become standard terminology—"the inability to mourn."

There is no escaping the fact that the events of 50 years ago are becoming less and less important for most people. The average German today is more concerned with the reality of the shipwrecked East German state and the crimes committed in the name of progress and socialism. The memory of Hitler's Germany is fading by the minute. And, indeed, that is only to be expected. Why, I sometimes ask myself, should a German born after 1945 torment himself for something he can no longer change, one way or the other? After all, the Nazi state is a thing of the past, and there is no way to undo the crimes of the fathers.

It is more difficult for a Jew who decides to stay in Germany. He is faced by two problems that are indirectly related to one another but are not necessarily regarded as being interconnected. First of all, someone like myself realizes very quickly that he is being pushed into the defensive, namely by the Jewish world outside Germany, which finds it difficult to accept the fact that there are Jews who are willing to live in post-Holocaust Germany.

I can cite a number of very typical experiences to back this up. I can still see the incredulous faces when I appeared in public abroad and said I was Jewish and came from Germany. This statement, which was admittedly made so nonchalantly that it sounded almost provocative, not infrequently met with heated reactions. I remember some turbulent lectures, especially in the United States during the 1970s, in which angry listeners jumped up and left the hall in protest. They did not understand, nor, presumably, did they want to understand, that after all the horrible things that had happened in Germany, Jews could live there again—in the "land of murderers," as they called Germany with a tone of disgust in their voices.

The other difficulty for someone who decides to stay in Germany is the diffuse feeling of guilt about living in the country which was the source of the most heinous mass murder of Jews in history. Many suffer from this. Yet they remain, not because they have no means of finding another country where they could live and have a family, but because they have made their peace with Germany and learned to live with it. Paradoxically, the inner torment for some has even become a kind of justification for staying.

Although, as an historian, I have learned to place a critical distance between myself and the historical events I am observing, I know that I will not be able to get away so quickly from Hitler and the consequences of Nazi dictatorship. The memory persists. Auschwitz, the metaphor for the organized murder of the Jews, is not "history which passes with time," but the tormenting here-and-now. There is no way to escape it. The images of the emaciated figures in the camps, the expressionless faces and the knowledge that millions of innocent people were murdered cannot be repressed. That is when I think of those who lost their lives, that is when I automatically and invariably also think of those members of my own family who were murdered, of my grandfather, who died in Theresienstadt and my grandmother, who was gassed in Auschwitz. This knowledge will torment me to the end of my days.

Yiddish Culture—A Soul Survivor of East Germany

by Jalda Rebling

The red brick Gethsemane Church in front of my window nearly disappears behind the sumptuous green of the old linden trees. In these warm, light-filled days, even the crumbling façades on the other side of the street have a friendly look about them, and if you take your bike out for an evening ride you will see lots of people sitting outside. This dirty, fragmented city becomes cozy, intimate. I like living here.

Since October 1989, when dissatisfaction with the situation in East Germany had reached the point where people took to the streets, my contact with this parish community has become extremely close. On October 8, Erev Yom Kippur, I came out of the synagogue to find that our neighborhood had been cordoned off yet again by a huge detachment of police: the non-violent had rebelled against violence. On the evening of October 9, after the end of Yom Kippur, I sang in the overcrowded Gethsemane Church, and when we came out, peace reigned. The power of the state had been broken. I had never experienced such celebration as I did that night, in this little street in the middle of East Berlin.

And whenever a German-nationalistic neighbor was particularly unpleasant to me, a Jewish woman, the Christian parish of Gethsemane was close by, but the Jewish congregation on the other side of the Brandenburg Gate was far away. "A good neighbor is always better than a distant relative," writes Scholem Asch.

This was again borne out right after the attacks in Hoyerswerda, the first pogrom-like rampages against foreigners after the Wall came down. Feeling utterly helpless, I happened to run into the arms of my neighbor, the pastor of Gethsemane Church:

"We must do something to show where we stand," I said.

"Alright, make a suggestion," he replied.

"I don't know—barricade the Schönhauser Allee at 5 o'clock in the afternoon, maybe."

"Alright, let's do it."

Two days later, at 5 o'clock in the afternoon, about 200 of us blocked off the Schönhauser Allee, one of the largest thoroughfares in Berlin, three times for five minutes.

It showed where we stood.

But that does not mean the "distant relative" is not important to me. Even in the late 1980s, the little hall where we held services for our East Berlin Jewish Community at Oranienburgerstrasse 28a became an important meeting place in this city. Today, it houses the kitchen of the OREN restaurant, where I like to go and eat falaffel when the weather is warm. The New Synagogue is right next-door, the one that was rebuilt, with the big gold cupola. It has an attractive lecture hall, an auditorium, and the library of the former East Berlin Community is housed there. It will become a meeting place for Jewish culture. Around the corner, in Grosse Hamburger Strasse, there is once again a Jewish school. Twenty-five years ago, when it was still a public vocational training college, I enrolled in a typing course there. Next year, in this old school founded by Moses Mendelssohn, my youngest son will learn the Hebrew Aleph-Bet and the Latin alphabet. A second kosher shop will soon be opened up in this area. The Jewish Culture Society (Jüdischer Kulturverein) is just a few steps away, at Monbijouplatz.

When we held our concerts with Jewish music, for many East Germans it was the first time they had been told anything about Israel. "Everyone knows about you here," the Israeli consul said after his first few hardworking months in the five new eastern states of the extended Federal Republic.

It was above all Christians who preserved the traces of Judaism in East Germany, and this often brought upon them the wrath, and only rarely earned the support, of the government. The Jewish communities, on the other hand, received sizeable support from the East German government, especially during the later years of the regime. The anti-fascist tradition was taken very seriously, but of course no one could be forced to embrace it. The growing contradiction between ideals and social reality drove many members of my generation to despair. Whereas, after the war, many Jewish emigrés made a conscious decision, filled with high ideals, to live in the newly founded German Democratic Republic, and in many cases sacrificed their Jewish identity for Communist dreams, many of their children made their way back to the Jewish community in the 1980s. And frequently it was not long before they brought their parents along with them. This group led to the emergence of the Jewish Culture Society, which is a source of enrichment for Jewish life in the center of Berlin. The small East Berlin Jewish Community was extremely important for us in East Germany, so sometimes it makes me very sad when I think that it folded within a matter of days in 1990, after the two Germanies become one again.

On November 9, 1990, when a large, official ceremony was held in our synagogue in Rykestrasse (in the Prenzlauer Berg district of Berlin) to commemorate the pogrom of the *Kristallnacht*,* the speakers included the president of the German parliament, the long-standing chairman (since deceased) of the West Berlin Community, the president of the (Western) Academy of the Arts and the rabbi of the West Berlin Community, whose wonderful hazan sang for the occasion. However, those who had filled this synagogue with Jewish life, Shabbat after Shabbat, for decades, were reduced to the role of showing the guests around the house, holding doors open for them and being spectators.

On that same November evening, we remembered *Kristall-*

nacht in our own way at the Gethsemane Church. A journalist had researched the history of a Jewish family who had lived in hiding for months in 1943–44 in the vicarage of the Gethsemane parish. Giora Feidman was our guest and played together with local musicians from East Berlin, members of a group of musicians and writers devoted to the intensive and committed study of Yiddish culture who had been meeting there for years.

Since January 1987, a Yiddish Culture Festival has been held here in Prenzlauer Berg every year. Before that, I had met wonderful performers from Israel, the United States, France, Sweden and Austria at international Yiddish festivals. But there were no artists from Warsaw, Bucharest, Vilnius or Chernovtsy, from those areas where Yiddish was once at home. This absence led to the idea of organizing a Yiddish Festival in Berlin.

However, it was to take more than two years to overcome all of the hurdles. Not only the government was skeptical, but also the chairman of the Association of Jewish Communities in East Germany. Yet, there were many people in East Berlin—performers, translators and publishers, most of whom were not Jewish—who were doing their best to make our "mameloshn," our Yiddish, understandable.

And finally it did work—on the 42nd anniversary of the liberation from Auschwitz, on January 27, 1987. We gave the festival the title "*dos lid is geblibn*" (the song has remained) and added "attempt at rapprochement" as a subtitle, since we, unlike our American colleagues, had nothing to "revive."

In those days there was no need to go in for costly publicity campaigns—a short announcement in the local newspaper *Berliner Zeitung* was all it took to let the people of Berlin know the event was happening. Then, when the correspondent from a West German television station expressed an interest in covering it, panic broke out at the cultural affairs department in charge. Three days before the festival was scheduled to begin, the authorities wanted to prohibit the whole thing, ostensibly because "there is no such thing as Yiddish culture . . ."

"Ber Halpern, is that an American Jew?" I was asked hysterically.

"No!" I said over the phone to a man I did not know. "He is a Soviet Yiddish poet!" Silence at the other end. We did not mention Halpern's fate in the Gulag until later, in the packed theater, with the cameras running.

The fact that this festival has kept going over the years is due to a series of miracles. In 1988, the leadership of the German Democratic Republic discovered an interest in all things Jewish, since, after all, Erich Honecker wanted to make a trip to the United States and had confidence in the "Jewish lobby." Our festival became a UNESCO contribution to the World Decade for Cultural Development, and suddenly many doors—and purses—were being opened for us. We were able to invite guests from Warsaw, Bucharest, Vilnius and Chernovtsy, and dreamed of having our festival become a place where East and West could come together.

Then, when the Wall finally came down in 1989, we thought: the world is open to everyone now, and we are no match for the kind of big Jewish festival that can be organized by the West Berlin Jewish Community, so we might as well pack up and go home. But we hadn't reckoned with our audience, who, like the press, put up quite a protest and said we should go on. But how? There were no institutions left which we could expect to provide the funding. Many would-be sponsors came and promised to give us assistance, but were never seen or heard from again. In October 1990, a letter arrived from the UNESCO Commission in Bonn, which made a modest sum available just to make it possible for anything to be held at all. The Yiddish scene in East Berlin had progressed so much in the preceding years that it was not hard for us to put together an interesting program without foreign guests. These wonderful musicians have shown once again, not least of all by their success in Israel and the United States, that Jewish music can be played very well by non-Jewish musicians. For us it is important to offer a genuine encounter with the remaining traces of this culture as a counterbalance to the distorted and kitschy Anatevka ("Fiddler on the Roof") image of eastern European Jewry that is so popular, not only in Germany.

In 1990, hundreds of Jewish immigrants from the Soviet Union came to Germany—a paradox in the tragic Jewish history of our century. We gladly placed our large hall at the disposal of the newly arrived Jewish artists, who included both classical and popular musicians, for an evening. Their concert was a huge success. In Germany, people like to hold speeches of mourning for the dead Jews, but here were living Jews who needed help.

The Yiddish Festivals have been supported by the Berlin Office of Cultural Affairs and by the German Federal Ministry of the Interior since 1992. The large exhibition entitled "Jewish Worlds," which was accompanied by a well-researched and comprehensive program of events, was held in Berlin. Yet, we were the only ones who upheld the memory of the Soviet Yiddish poets who were murdered on August 12, 1952. Polish Jewry was the focus of our festival in 1993, and Romanian Jewry in 1994.

Because of the tense financial situation in Berlin, the last festival was saved only because Berlin's senator for cultural affairs became personally involved after we told him how important it was for this little festival to be preserved. After many failed attempts, we have finally been able to enlist the support of the Berlin Jewish Community. Until 1989, we had worked together with our East Berlin Jewish Community, year after year, but only very few Jews west of the Brandenburg Gate had taken any notice of our work.

A dream has come true: our festival has indeed become a place where East and West come together.

In January 1995, scholars and artists from Lithuania, Israel and New York will be joining us to celebrate the 50th anniversary of the liberation from Auschwitz. It will be our Ninth Annual Yiddish Festival, opened by the world-famous *Kapelye* from New York—something we could only have dreamed of back in 1987. A miracle?

For me, Yiddish songs and literature are the *heimishkeit* I will always be searching for in vain, since it was lost with my family in Auschwitz. Only five people came back.

I love the wonderful songs and ballads of the Sephardic Jews. In Germany, unfortunately, they are virtually unknown. In Amsterdam, the city of my birth, Ashkenazim and Sephardim have been living together for hundreds of years.

German-Jewish music and history, in turn, are part of the culture in which I live.

Am I torn? Perhaps. Or rather, yes, of course. That's part of being Jewish.

In Communist East Germany it was not possible for me to become a "normal" member of society, although I tried very hard.

When I moved up here to Prenzlauer Berg in 1988, it was the first time I was not looked upon and treated by my neighbors like some exotic bird. Everyone here is accepted the way they are. I have found friends here who have remained true to themselves, amidst the shift in political worlds. There are people here for whom my songs and my work are important. There were so many times when I wanted to get out of East Germany! Whenever we were allowed to go to concerts in the West, I always dreaded the moment when the border gate was closed tightly behind me again. The feeling of not being free to leave whenever I wanted often gave me sleepless nights. I am sure this paranoia in me is thousands of years old. But wouldn't it follow me everywhere I went? When you go away, don't you take yourself and all of your fears with you? Thomas Brasch, another of us children of Jewish emigrés who did not get along with East Germany, once wrote:

"Where I die I do not want to go: I want to stay where I have never been."

And today he writes:

"The alternative is no longer one of where to escape to, but of where not to stay."

We already saw the new Nazis taking shape in former East Germany, but people laughed off my warnings at the time.

Since 1977–78 or thereabouts, the level of interest in the Shoah★ has been growing in Germany, and thus an interest in Yiddish culture. On the other hand, however, we have also witnessed the growth of a dangerous fascination with the stories that grandfathers tell about the "good old days" of their youth, when "Germany was big and powerful." Communist East Germany's anti-fascist education, which was becoming increasingly formalistic, could do little to stem the tide. Would it have helped to prohibit such sentiments? We have found out all too well how ineffective bans are. Many of those who are now looking for simplistic solutions and the ideals of their childhood again were once well-behaved Young Pioneers and members of the Free German Youth, the official East German youth organizations. They wear uniforms today just like their militant-socialist parents did. The uniforms may have changed, but the mentality is the same. But the violent gangs are only the conspicuous tip of the iceberg. As I see it, the real danger lies in the way people are growing accustomed to such brutality, in the way that violence is becoming socially acceptable. More and more people seem to be trying to "put history behind us at last." If these people had their way, memorials to those who died in concentration camps would disappear altogether or be reduced to memorials to everyone, to "the victims of tyranny" in general, since the innocent German victims after liberation on May 8, 1945, should also be remembered. It is extremely difficult for a nation to live with a history such as Germany's. Germans are still busy repressing memories of the past.

As for myself, however, remembering through songs is the only way I can live with the profound pain and nightmares. I am afraid that, once the ceremonies commemorating the 50th anniversary of liberation have come and gone, we and our eternal warnings will be left over like living fossils from a pre-historic age. An American pastor once asked me whether I am not beginning to get tired of these never-ending Holocaust discussions. An increasing number of people come up to us after our concerts to tell us how nice the music was, but ask when will we ever "let bygones be bygones?" The press is really playing up those attacks, they say; anti-Semitism is definitely a thing of the past.

Yet how can the pain of the Shoah ever come to rest? Will we and our children ever be able to live out the rest of our lives in a normal way and carry our millennia-old history forward?

In 1992, the town of Sternberg in Mecklenburg-Western Pomerania honored the memory of 25 Jews who had been killed there in 1492. The Protestant pastor and his wife carefully prepared a whole series of events to commemorate this day. Meanwhile, however, French Jews were under arrest in Rostock (about 50 km away from Sternberg) because they had "illegally" attempted to mount a plaque commemorating a pogrom in the Lichtenhagen district of Rostock where a home for asylum-seekers in a densely populated residential area was suddenly ablaze and no one lifted a finger to help. A few days later, the French Jews were deported to France as "undesirable aliens" without any information being released to the press.

On the day of the official ceremony, the head of the district administration, the Catholic bishop, the Protestant bishop and the mayor delivered emotional speeches about the Jews who had been killed there 500 years before. We were invited to provide the musical accompaniment for the *Gedenkfeier*—a strange German word meaning "commemorative celebration." After the third speaker had finished, I was overcome with anger and asked why no one was talking about the Jews who were alive and sitting in jail, or about the dangerous situation in Germany. The rabbi from Hannover was the first to put this whole event back on an even keel with a few wise words. But later, in the evening, there was a concert in the very cold Sternberg church. We sang Jewish songs, and so did a Berlin hazan. Afterward, while we were drinking tea to warm up in the parish kitchen and got to talking about topical issues in German politics, the Berlin cantor said that the problem for Germany was the "asylum-seekers" and that the borders should finally be closed—the boat was full.

Speechless, I stood up, said goodbye and drove back to Berlin.

I would not say that I have complete faith in democracy, but it seems to be the only chance we have at the moment. I hope it will stay strong enough to resist the unmistakable dangers in Europe as a whole. I put my faith in my friends in the neighborhood and all over the world.

I like living here with the red-brick Gethsemane Church and the old trees in front of my window, and my three sons are turning out to be real Berliners.

Germany—Home Sweet Home?

by Richard C. Schneider

Jews have no business living in Germany—this has been the premise underlying Jewish life in Germany since 1945. It applies to the Central Council of Jews in Germany, to the Jewish communities, to every single Jewish individual. And, naturally, it also applies to me. That is what Germans think and so do Jews, everywhere in the world. It was a mistake for Jews to settle in Germany. It undermined the self-esteem of the Jewish community even more than the Nazis succeeded in doing in the ghettos, the concentration camps and the death camps. Nazi Germany had killed six million Jews—murdered, slaughtered, annihilated and gassed them—and yet, only a short time after this, the greatest catastrophe in human history, Jews were making their home in the country of the murderers, living side by side, wall to wall, with the very same people who had been accomplices, Wehrmacht soldiers, murderers, SS officers, party members and concentration camp guards.

Mother, Father—how could you have possibly done this? What on earth was going on in your souls that you could bring yourselves to bear such a thing? How much did you have to force yourselves to forget in order to endure the day-to-day humiliation, the torture of it? Or was that nothing compared to what you had already been through? Could it be that, after Auschwitz and Treblinka, after Maidanek and Sobibor, after Dachau, Bergen-Belsen, Mauthausen and Ravensbrück, it simply no longer makes any difference where one lives? How one lives?

These are the questions we asked our parents—sometimes only in our minds, however, because we did not dare to touch this wound. Or because we did not want to hear the answer, did not want to know the truth.

Yet this deep-seated feeling of guilt, the conviction that Jews should not live in Germany after the Shoah* was branded into our souls just as the concentration camp numbers were once branded into the forearms of our parents and grandparents.

But now we are simply here, in Germany. There is already a third generation, and a fourth will soon be born. And on top of it all, Jews are now migrating to Germany from eastern Europe, not to mention the Israelis who have been living here for decades.

Jews are living in Germany: they lived here in the Middle Ages and in 1933, they lived here in 1945, and they are still here today. That's the way it is.

The Germans have to live with it. And so do we Jews.

But what is Jewish identity in Germany? What does it mean to be a Jew in Germany?

The question of Jewish identity is one that is being asked of Jews all over the world in this secular age, so in that sense it seems to be nothing out of the ordinary. Yet here in Germany the question assumes additional weight. Nowhere in the world do Jews live with such serious ruptures in their soul as they do in Germany, nowhere is their identity as questionable as it is here, since for those of us born after the war it already means being "German" again to some extent. Jews in Germany live with guilt feelings and excuses, with self-doubt and obstinacy, with a guilt complex and pride, with thousands of good reasons for living here of all places, although they know that all of those reasons are flimsy. Unlike our parents, those of us who were born after 1945 have a choice. We can leave this country any time we like; the borders are open, we are young, healthy, multilingual. But this country is our birthplace, our home, whether we care to admit it or not. Sometimes we

93

have a sneaking feeling that, faced with the growth of neo-Nazism, we are making the same mistakes as German Jews did before 1933, who also believed—and for much better reasons than we do today—that this country was their ancestral home. Jews in Germany live with an ever-present past and an ever less certain future.

Jews should not be living in Germany, it is said. But they are here. For that reason, there are specific, complex features to Jewish life in this country which epitomize the ambiguities of the Diaspora.

The degree to which former West Germany was a home, albeit a problematic one, did not become clear to us all until Germany was reunited. No one ever seriously thought that they would live to see the day when the two Germanies would be one again. Not even the West German politicians seriously believed it would happen, even though they formally paid lip service to national unity. We Jews certainly had no interest in seeing it happen—not so much because of a lack of loyalty to this state, but because of muted fears in every one of us at the prospect of a large and powerful Germany. West Germany was a provisional arrangement, and this suited us only too well, it was just as provisional as our own lives were in this country: already long established and manifest, but still somehow inchoate, a sort of intermediate stage "between worlds" that felt comfortable, a status quo in which one could feel at ease, despite all the reservations and justified doubts one felt about it. Firmly anchored in the Western alliance, insignificant in foreign policy, Allied troops on German soil—all of this was a guarantee of democratic stability that we had no reason to doubt.

As a young man living here in Munich—in Bavaria, where U.S. troops had been stationed since the end of the war—I used to listen to nothing but the American Forces Network all day long. For me, AFN was not just the radio station where Wolfman Jack played the hottest sounds from the world of rock and pop, or where the DJ read American football scores.

94

The U.S. army station was the only one I listened to, like everyone else in my generation. To me, AFN meant freedom, the gateway to the big wide world, the spark of hope that showed the Germans the way out of their Nazi past, proof of the fact that a liberal, open-minded way of life was also possible within Germany. And, at the same time, it was a quiet indication of the fact that, despite the close season on Jews, the taboo and the protective shield that existed in Germany, a Jew's freedom was to be found elsewhere.

Freedom that was not won in struggle—how can anyone possibly appreciate what that is really worth? My generation certainly cannot. This generation of Germans who, as children of the perpetrators, also grew up between remembering and repression, who preach a peculiar breed of pacifism which has more to do with not getting involved than with any genuine sense of inner conviction—they could not be trusted. Regardless of whether it was the left-wing terrorist Rote Armee Fraktion (Red Army Faction) or the Green Movement, whether it was Nicaragua, "Palestine" or South Africa—all of that political activism was just so much eyewash. The conservative forces calmly and steadily continued to shape this republic just the way they wanted. I can already hear the howls of protest from the left, and I also know the arguments that will be hurled at me—about how much the protest movement of 1968 did to change the political climate in West Germany. And maybe it did, but in the meantime all I can do is shrug my shoulders. The fact remains that in Germany the revolution took place within narrow confines. The current political situation is proof of that, unfortunately. Never since 1945 has Germany been faced by such an immediate threat from the right, never has right-wing extremism been as much on the rise as it is today. So, what was achieved by the flower-power generation, what emerged from it?

When I began working as a journalist, I had a pressing need to deal intensively and publicly with the problem of German-

Jewish relations. I began writing about the subject, doing radio and TV broadcasts and going to symposia and conferences. In the process I discovered that, strangely enough, I was one of the few Jews from my generation to come forward in public. Micha Brumlik, Henryk M. Broder, Lea Fleischmann, Michael Wolffsohn and all of the other Jewish figureheads of the German media are now pushing 50. Those of us in my generation, who will soon be 40, however, seem to have lost our voices. We do not make ourselves heard to the same degree as our older "sisters and brothers." We all belong to the second generation. However, whereas many of our older brothers and sisters were born abroad—Broder was born in Poland, Wolffsohn in Israel—and did not come to Germany until early childhood, nearly all of us younger ones were born here.

That distinction has led to completely different ways of looking at things, and it has also most certainly changed our attitudes toward this country. Does that mean that we "youngsters" can simply declare, in a takeoff on John F. Kennedy's famous line "*Ich bin ein Berliner*," "*Ich bin ein Bundesrepublikaner*"—I am a citizen of the Federal Republic of Germany?

I think we can. But we, too, still bear the marks of a broken identity. For, although I was born in Germany, I only gradually went through the stages which established my identity as someone who belongs in that country, at least from an external point of view. My parents, who after all were East European refugees, did not apply for German citizenship for many years. So that made me a "stateless person" as well, a term which was completely absurd when applied to myself and many other Jewish friends of mine. My parents said the main reason for their reluctance to acquire German citizenship was that they were afraid I might be drafted into the German army if they did. A prospect which was unbearable for them. Their son in a German uniform! Although there was a decree which exempted the children of those who had been persecuted under the Nazis for religious or political reasons from serving in the Bundeswehr, my parents were not so sure that this decree would still be valid when I turned eighteen.

So I remained a "stateless person" for just under 23 years. And when I finally decided to become a German citizen, I had to go through a long and tedious procedure in order to explain why I now wanted to do so. I had to say something about my sense of belonging to German culture, and also state that I did not feel as if I belonged to my parents' culture at all. Fortunately, I was studying German language and literature, a point in my favor. My lawyer, the woman who processed my application for citizenship, even gave me the tip, just in case I had to take a language test, that, whatever I did, I should not say that I knew any foreign languages, or only English at most, but definitely not Hungarian, and least of all Hebrew! Maybe this advice was nonsense and would not have had any bearing on the authorities' decision, but it was interesting in the sense that, based on a thorough knowledge of German authorities and bureaucrats, someone felt it was a way of eliminating any problems right from the start: as if to say, anyone who wants to become a German citizen had better not know any foreign languages. Here was a prejudice of Adolf Hitler's winding its way to the surface again. He mistrusted all interpreters because he felt that anyone who could speak more than one language could no longer be loyal.

But naturalization did not mean that my problems were over, not by a long shot. The fact is, the ambivalence of my own feelings became immeasurable when I was given my German passport at the counter, opened it up and read the sentence on the first page: "The bearer of this passport is German." My grandfather would have turned over in his grave at that moment, had he not gone up in smoke at Auschwitz. It was a moment of shame vis-à-vis my ancestors who had died in the gas chambers, a moment when I felt I had betrayed them. I was overcome by the strongest feeling of sorrow. I stood there as if stunned in the midst of the people who were pushing from one counter to the next. I was suddenly seized by the pressing need to run back to the nice official and tell her that it had all been a misunderstanding and that I would really rather have my old passport back, that being a "stateless person" was much more in tune with my emotional situation. But there I was, gingerly holding my new green passport in my fingertips and feeling like the victim of a split-second metamorphosis that I would never be able to reverse. I had stamped my own mark of Cain on my forehead. Everyone outside of Germany would now see that I am German. "But I'm not" was what I would now have to call out for all of eternity. And what would the Israeli customs officials at Tel Aviv airport think? "Aha, another Nazi child, coming here trying to salve his conscience!"

There were several reasons for my decision to apply for German citizenship. The first was pragmatic. As a "stateless person" I did not have to do military service, but I did not have the right to vote either. I also had to have my passport renewed every two years by the German authorities. At some point, this situation got on my nerves. I needed a visa for every little trip to Austria or wherever, and the German customs officials eyed me with suspicion at every border crossing. When I was in my early twenties, the left-wing radical Baader-Meinhof gang was at the height of its terrorist activity. So a young man with a name that sounded as German as mine was automatically suspect if he suddenly pulled out his "jeans passport," as we Jews called it because of the color.

But there was certainly also an idealistic reason for my wanting to become a German citizen. This country was my country, it was where I was born. I wanted to get rid of this status of someone without a nationality. It was a product of World War II and had nothing more to do with me and my reality. It might have been appropriate to my parents, but for me it made no sense. That is perhaps the most important difference between ourselves and our older brothers and sisters. For us, West Germany was already a natural quantity in our lives. It was the only thing we had ever known. We were no longer immigrants.

There is no doubt whatsoever that I feel attached to this country, that I am rooted here in a way that I am reluctant to admit, even to myself.

Let's take the Germans' favorite sport—soccer—for example. I was a little boy in 1966, when Germany was playing against England in the World Cup Final at Wembley Stadium. Shortly before the end of normal playing time, England was leading 2:1. I was on the verge of a nervous breakdown, could barely hold back the tears, and kept asking my parents, who were also watching the match, whether Germany still had a chance of winning. My mother calmed me down, said she was sure Germany would score another goal, I did not have to worry. Then, when the Germans equalized just before the final whistle, I let out a whoop of jubilation, rampaged up and down the living room, crying and laughing at the same time, and it was all my parents could do to calm me down. And in the end, when the Germans lost 4:2 after extra time, I was heartbroken. I wonder how my parents must have felt to see my enthusiasm for Germany. I never dared to ask them. When Germany won the World Cup again in 1974—that time the German team was playing Holland in Munich—I was again overjoyed, but by this time victory had acquired a slightly bittersweet taste: the Dutch were a liberal people, and many of them had tried to help the Jews during the Nazi occupation. And then came 1990: another World Cup victory. This time it was no longer just a matter of winning a soccer tournament, but a demonstration of national grandeur. On top of it all, Germany was to be re-united in the fall: "*Deutschland, Deutschland über alles*" was the motto of that year. I could no longer feel happy about it at all. The gradual decline in my ability to get excited about my "home" team ran parallel to my increasing awareness of the German-Jewish problem. Actually, nothing would be more natural than to feel at home where you grow up. But history

99

refuses to go away. We are stuck in the middle of it, and since reunification more so than ever.

Reunification marked the beginning of a "normalization process" the full force of which is being felt by the second generation in particular. On the one hand, coming to terms with the ever virulent anti-Semitism in postwar Germany had proved to be aggravating and nerve-wracking. I soon knew by heart all of the other side's stupid and false arguments. But in a certain respect we had grown "accustomed" to this ritual. It was part of being a Jew in Germany. At the same time discussions of this type turned out to be completely meaningless, since the so-called German-Jewish dialogue, as people like to call this perfumed mealy-mouthing at "well-intentioned" events, is usually hypocritical. In the meantime I have grown tired of the suspicion that is hidden behind the friendly faces, the aggravation over the fact that my mere existence as a Jew always reminds my German counterpart of his sinister history.

Anti-Semitism has become socially acceptable in Germany again. It has found its way into normal conversation, no one has qualms about venting anti-Jewish feelings openly. In that sense, we are returning to a situation which Jews have known for thousands of years. Only we of the second generation born in Germany do not know it—and that is the point. The fact that anti-Jewish sentiments—just like xenophobia—are no longer being voiced in whispers at least gives us the advantage of knowing right away who our enemies are. But it also offers this society a perfect opportunity to come to terms with its own evils in such a way that they can be pulled out of the deepest German soil by the roots.

A rift seems to be opening up for us Jews. OK, we are German citizens—so what should we do? This is a rhetorical question, of course, but it is meant to be taken seriously in that it brings up the issue of loyalty to this state, a state that is becoming less and less dependable.

The dilemma is not new: the question of "belonging" in the "host country" is an old problem which the Jewish Diaspora has had to answer in different ways over and over again. But precisely at this time, in this Germany, the dilemma is almost irresolvable, because all of the models have long since been tried out, and most of them—as history has shown—are doomed to failure. Once again, Jews have gone on the defensive. Yet, going on the defensive—reacting rather than acting—is the foremost characteristic of the failed Diaspora. This is what always happens when the Jews themselves attach to the term "Jew" only the political and social meaning that reflects its function in relation to the non-Jewish outside world, but no longer the religious meaning that it has in a purely Jewish context. When that happens, Jews allow others to take over the reins, and no longer have a part in history, their own history. Taking a part in history means acting of one's own accord and not merely reacting as a potential victim. The Shoah★ as an identity-giving characteristic of Jewishness: this attitude in Germany is partly responsible for the desolate situation in the Jewish community. This perverted form of Jewishness also exists in the United States, but here in Germany it is one we can afford even less than in other places in the world; for it would mean once again allowing the Germans to tell us who and what a Jew is.

Adapted from: Richard Chaim Schneider, *Zwischenwelten. Ein jüdisches Leben im heutigen Deutschland* (Munich: Kindler Verlag, 1994), 318 pages.

Jewish Identity—
An East German Dimension

by Wolf Biermann

The following article was written by the poet and singer Wolf Biermann in the form of a letter to his close friend Ellen Presser, director of the Youth and Culture Center of the Jewish Community in Munich.

Altona, November 14, 1994

My dear Ellen,

So now you want me, of all people, to come up with a piece for your friend's book—and at short notice, too. But what do I know that would be worth telling about what's left of the Jews in this fragmented place called Germany? The only story I might have to tell is why I never really became a Jew.

And because I'm not a Jew, I don't really belong in this book. I was not graced with being born Jewish, that is, not in the eyes of Orthodox Jewish law. I was only dis-graced by being born Jewish in the eyes of the Nuremberg Laws★.

According to the Nazis' patriarchal legal standards, I at least qualified as a "first-grade half-breed." So Herr Hitler in Berlin found me more Jewish than the rabbinate in Jerusalem did. And what I search for and find in myself is irrelevant for both sides. What absurd categories! "*I will be the one to decide who is Jewish!*" This Viennese curse which Göring made so despicably popular can still to this day occasionally be heard from some foul-mouthed anti-Semite, but could just as easily come from the mouths of Jews who live in the tradition.

Did I ever tell you that my father was not originally sent to a concentration camp as a Jew, but was put in jail for being a Communist worker and resistance fighter? In 1933, when my father stood trial in Hamburg for the first time for illegally printing the Communist party newspaper, he piped up and corrected the judge who had asked him the routine questions as to his name and occupation and address and religion. This is what the judge dictated to the court stenographer for the record: Dagobert Biermann, toolmaker and fitter, born November 13, 1904, in Hamburg, no religion. At that, my father jumped up and shouted obstinately: "I'm Jewish!" My father got out of jail two years later, I was born in November 1936, and he had exactly three more months to enjoy before he was arrested again—and this time he was sentenced to six years for high treason. So he was relatively safe in prison in the Oslebshausen district of Bremen. In February 1943, the Nazis obviously "cleansed" the jails of Jews, too, which meant that my father had to exchange the prison cell where he might have survived until 1945 for the gas chamber in Auschwitz. You know the lines from my song:

Ich bleibe, was ich immer war
Halb Judenbalg und halb ein Goj
Nur eines weiß ich klipp und klar:
Nur wer sich ändert, bleibt sich treu . . .

(I remain what I always was
Half Jew-brat and half goy
But one thing I know for sure:
Only someone who changes remains true to himself . . .)

My mother complained until the day she died: he was so smart, why did he have to be so dumb! Why did your father have to say that, without being asked, they might not even have noticed that he also happened to be a Jew, they would have forgotten about it, he might still be alive today . . .

103

It was the Nazis, of all people, who made the Communist dockyard worker Dagobert "Israel" Biermann into an Israelite again. The same thing happened to a fair number of assimilated Jews. All water under the bridge now, dear Ellen, the blood of yesteryear, a few tears left over from the thousand-year Reich.

Today is a quiet Sunday, we've had a pleasant breakfast with David and Lukas, our two youngsters. I lit two candles and told the boys that their Grandpa would have been 90 years old this very day . . . and showed them the young, darkhaired man on the old photos in our kitchen. Hanging next to it are photos of my father's mother, Louise, his brother Karl, his sister Rosi, the whole mishpokhe.

Everyone in my family who could have made a Jew out of me, in the spiritual sense, had already been deported from Hamburg to Minsk in 1941 and every single one of them was murdered.

But because I swam against the current of the millions of westward-bound refugees by going east in 1953—I was 16 years old at the time—to the "fatherland of all working people," I went through another process of de-Jewification, this time in the German Democratic Republic [East Germany or the GDR]:

The fact is, the sad remains of Jewishness which my mother had instilled in me out of love for my father then withered and dried up once and for all in the deserts of Stalinism.

There was no open hatred of Jews in the GDR, but there did exist a subcutaneous form of anti-Semitism. The apparatschiks' distrust of Jews and the fear of their cosmopolitanism were always at work in the minds of the Bolshevist party linetoers. Anti-Semitism was "dirty" in the Eastern bloc countries and was only officially tolerated if it appeared in the guise of "clean" anti-Zionism. The fact that Jews were accused of petty-bourgeois Zionist nationalism and of cosmopolitanism at the same time was a hypocritical illogicality which was foisted on us as higher dialectics.

But, as I said: Whereas Stalin prepared the Soviet final solution to the Jewish question shortly before his death, his East German quislings were not as brash about it as he was. The West was embarrassingly close, the border to West Germany was much too exposed, the feelings of shock and shame on the part of many decent Germans over the genocide were still too fresh. Besides, hardly any Jews had survived in Germany to kindle the murderers' imagination.

Of the few Jews who came back from emigration, not very many went to the GDR. There were Jewish Communists who came out of "right" emigration in the East and "wrong" exile in the West. All of those in the nomenklatura who had fought in the Spanish Civil War were regarded with misgivings and mistrust by the cadre guards. The Slanski trial, the Rajk trial. Gerhard Eisler, Hanns Eisler's brother, would be sacrificed on the altar of anti-Titoism. Especially when they became higher-level functionaries of the SED [East Germany's ruling Communist Party], the Jews repressed their Jewishness or were especially anxious to keep proving that, as far as they were concerned, everything that was Jewish was obsolete and unimportant, or even objectionable.

Now that I'm doing my best to remember, a few GDR Jews do come to mind. Stefan Heym, the de-Jewified Jew, who, now that his world has collapsed, is whoring around in the bed of the Party of Democratic Socialism [successor to the former East German Communist Party] with the criminals from the now powerless old regime, and all at once is very much a Jew and accuses us, his critics, of being anti-Semitic. Markus Wolf, one-time general in the dreaded Ministry for State Security and head of East German foreign intelligence, is also a Jew. His GDR systematically supported Israel's mortal enemies by training Iraqi officers in chemical warfare and serving as a base of operations for Arab terrorists.

I could tell you more about one Jew in the GDR—the lawyer Dr. Götz Berger. He looked as "Jewish" as Lion Feuchtwanger, he was a sweet, cultivated and upstanding human being and occasionally he vehemently denied that he was Jewish. Robert Havemann and I were friends with this man during the difficult years from 1965 on, after the regime had imposed a total ban on us. He fought in the Spanish Civil War—an old-guard Communist. But why am I telling you old stories? You are so young that you probably don't even know who Robert Havemann was. He was a professor of chemistry, and a philosopher, and he was my closest friend in those difficult years. I would have cracked up without him. And he was the first real Jew I had met in my life: a German giant with long blond Aryan legs—the exact opposite of a Jew. He looked like Schindler in Spielberg's film.

Havemann's father was one of those oh-so-refined Nazis who claimed their Nazism stood in the intellectual tradition of Goethe and Schiller. He threatened to report his son to the Gestapo during the 1930s if he did not stop his Communist nonsense right away. My friend Robert was condemned to death in 1943 by Freisler's "People's Court," was jailed alongside Honecker in Brandenburg, was liberated by the Red Army. After 1945, he became a big shot in the GDR—he didn't look so good in those days. But then he finally started sounding off again, he became a resistance fighter again, this time against the second—redwashed—dictatorship. This goy taught me my first Jewish jokes. And where had he learned them? From Jews he had hidden and saved in Berlin during the Nazi period. But now back to the Jewish lawyer:

After 1945, Götz Berger was a public prosecutor in the GDR for awhile, and now I hear that during those particularly sinister times he is supposed to have pushed through some sinister verdicts, including some death sentences pronounced upon innocent people.

Götz Berger later worked as a lawyer, was a member of the officially recognized association of lawyers in "Berlin, the capital city of the GDR"—in East Berlin, in other words. He, like us, was deeply shaken by the 20th Party Congress of the CPSU [Communist Party of the Soviet Union] in 1956. That

106

was when Khrushchev lifted for the first time a corner of the blood-stained cloth that concealed the Stalin era. The horrible truths of his secret speech did not, of course, remain a secret.

It came as a shattering blow to many honest old-guard Communists, and some of them resurrected the ethical motives of their youth, broke off their careers as senior party officials, began bucking the party line. Dr. Berger became our legal counsel, the lawyer who defended Robert Havemann against the chicanery of the powers-that-were. The position we took at that time was: Ulbricht and Honecker and Mielke are anti-Communists—and we are the true Communists. I think that was also the way this old Spanish Civil War veteran thought and felt.

After I was expatriated from the GDR in the gloomy month of November 1976, Götz Berger stood by my friend Robert Havemann even during his long years spent under house arrest. Despite his distinguished record of service to the GDR, the East German leadership stripped Berger of all his rights. As an old man, he lost his license to practice law, and was barred from pursuing his profession under a particularly insidious form of blacklisting. To replace him, the leadership forced my friend Havemann to accept as his appointed defense counsel a certain Dr. Gregor Gysi, accused today (correctly, I believe) of being the informer "Notary," a code name which has turned up in East German secret police [Stasi] files. Gysi was a shrewd newbreed operator and a product of the regime. This young dynamic upstart had even ascended in the party nomenklatura to the position of chairman of the so-called Assembly of Lawyers in East Berlin and secretary of the association of SED lawyers. But that is no longer talked about, now that the same Dr. Gysi is a member of the German parliament, party leader of the damnable PDS and darling of the talk shows on all the TV stations. Incidentally, he too is a Jew with only a Jewish father.

Robert Havemann died in 1983 at his house in Grünheide,

which was guarded around the clock. But Götz Berger lived to see the collapse of the GDR. When I gave my first concert in East Berlin shortly after the Wall was opened up, he came to the Kammerspiele of the Deutsches Theater. After the singing was over, I met him in the foyer and we embraced—it was a heartrendingly beautiful moment. But it was followed by the outburst which I want to tell you about because it is a perfect example to illustrate the embarrassing subject of Jewishness.

I said: Dear Götz, just think, I have made friends with an extremely interesting person—Arno Lustiger. You've got to meet him; he's a Polish Jew who survived Auschwitz and Buchenwald and even Langenstein, that horrendous concentration camp in the Harz mountains. On the death march of the 5,000 inmates from Auschwitz to Buchenwald, he half-carried an exhausted comrade, a man who had fought in the Spanish Civil War.

For weeks, on his plank bed in the concentration camp hut, this man from the International Brigades had told his strong, young friend about his experiences in the civil war against Franco. After a few days, Arno could not support the dying man any longer, and broke down himself. So the veteran wound up lying at the side of the road, where he was shot dead by the SS as they were going by. Since that time, however, the subject of Spain has continued to haunt my friend in Frankfurt, and now he has written a book which, for the first time, describes in great detail the tremendous role played by the Jews in the Spanish Civil War. Götz! You fought in Spain, too! You'll find it very moving. I can get the book for you, it's called *Shalom Libertad!*

At that, the old man screeched: "I don't give a shit about the Jews in the Spanish Civil War! And I don't want to read a book about the vegetarians in the Spanish Civil War either!" Then he left me standing there and went huffing and puffing down the stairs and out onto Schumannstrasse.

This angry outburst, by the way, had nothing to do with the old, familiar Jewish self-hatred. It was more like the last

108

bastion of Stalinism in this tired human breast. In other respects, Götz Berger had painfully freed himself of the shackles of totalitarian doctrine—but this feeling of "let me be anything, just not Jewish," was the final, the most deeply ingrained poison in his emotional and intellectual make-up.

Dear Ellen, to put it in plain and simple terms: The Nazis wiped out the Jewish people—but the Stalinists preferred to liquidate everything that was Jewish in the Jews.

I have given public readings of the Katzenelson poem on five occasions now. In the Hamburg theater, for my northern German fishheads, and for the Rhenish merrimakers in Cologne, and also in the elegant city of Munich and even in the Vienna Burgtheater. The very last two verses in the *Großer Gesang vom ausgerotteten jüdischen Volk*—the *Great Song of the Liquidated Jewish People*—go like this:

14

Und meine Kommunist'n, Hitzköpf! nie mehr machen die
    sich breit
Bekämpfen nie mehr meine treuen, freien Briderlech vom
    BUND
Ach Die! und Unsre! Dabei trugen beide gleich und stolz das
    Joch
Der Welt. Und jeder von uns hat gekämpft, gelitten und ge-
    strebt
Chaluzím, unsre Jungen haben an die Menschheit sich ver-
    schenkt
Verflucht hab ich so oft, daß ihr euch beißt wie Katz und
    Hund
Mit unsern Roten. Doch nun jammert mich das Ende dieses
    Streits
Denn würdet ihr noch streiten, wüßt ich wenigstens: Ihr lebt.

(And my Communists, hotheads! never again will they spread
    out and make themselves at home
Never again will they fight my loyal, free brothers from the
    BUND
Oh, Them! and Ours! Yet both of them shouldered the yoke
    of the world, equally and proudly. And each of us
    fought, suffered and strove
Chaluzím, our boys gave themselves away to humanity
I have so often cursed the fact that you bite each other like
    cats and dogs
with our Reds. But now I am tormented by the end of this
    dispute
For if you were still fighting, then at least I would know that
    you are still alive.)

15

Weh mir, da ist nicht keiner mehr . . .
    Und war mal 'n Volk.
        Vorbei!

Und ausgelöscht. . .
    ein ganzes Volk.
        Uns gibt es nun nicht mehr

Verflucht,
    was für'n Geschichtchen!
        Mit 'nem Bibelchen begann's

Von Moses steht's geschrieben
    —schönes Märchen,
        traurig, aber wahr—

Vom Kampf am Sinai
    mit Amalek
        bis hin zu unserm ärgsten Feind

Dem Deutschen.
    Gott! O weite Himmel,
        breite Erde, o gewaltig Meer

Vernichtet all die Schlechten . . .
    nicht auf dieser Erde!
        Laßt sie machen, ja:

Sie selber werden sich vernichten.
    Alle.
        Und für immerdar.

(Woe is me, no one is left . . .
    And once it was a people.
        Gone!

And extinguished . . .
    an entire people.
        Now we are no more.

Damnit,
    what a tale!
        It all started with a little Bible

Of Moses, it is written
    —a nice fairy tale,
        sad but true—

Of the battle at Sinai
    with Amalek
        all the way to our worst enemy

The German.
>   God! Oh spacious heaven,
>   vast earth, oh mighty ocean

Destroy all of the bad people . . .
>   not on this earth!
>   Let them do as they wish—yes:

They will destroy themselves.
>   All of them.
>   And forever.)

The Jewish people was totally annihilated, and yet it still exists. Katzenelson was right: the Nazis destroyed themselves and have still survived in the best of shape. In Israel I heard the complaint: There are more and more Israelis here and fewer and fewer Jews.

I am not Jewish and I have always been Jewish. The fissure runs straight down the middle. After my citizenship was taken away from me in 1976, I was an Easterner in the West and, since the GDR collapsed, I have been a Wessi [West German] for the Ossis [East Germans]. In my old GDR song "Und als wir ans Ufer kamen" (And when we came ashore), the refrain goes: "Ich möchte am liebsten weg sein / Und bleibe am liebsten hier . . ."—I wish I were gone / And would rather stay here . . . But since I was expatriated in 1976, I sing this song just the same way in the West, because it expresses an inner tension which every person knows who suffers in his country because he feels responsible. You know how it is, dear Ellen, everyone hates that part of humanity which he loves most. I could say: I am a Jew-brat and Communist child, I'm a victim so it's all the same to me, what do I care about these guilty Germans! And you could even say: What do I care about Germany, my parents are Polish Jews. And yet we still live in this country under the ashes and are still German and there's no getting around it.

A friend of mine in the GDR hid my old notebooks for 15 years, and after the Wall came down he gave each and every one of them back to me. Leafing through them I came across a funny four-liner, written in December 1962, in other words at the time of the obligatory Christmas market in East Berlin.

At this Eastern-bloc socialist Christmas market, the main attraction was roast chickens, which were called "broilers" in GDR German, and people ate socialist sausages, progressive pancakes and potato fritters that were loyal to the Party. There was revolutionary red-wine punch, gingerbread hearts that intoned the fight for peace, an old German carousel going around to modern, revamped Christmas songs. Sentimental German gemütlichkeit soup from the Communist gulash dispenser. You could buy educationally valuable war toys; model soldiers of the National People's Army and kitschy Christmas tree ornaments were also on sale. A little wooden Christmas angel made in the Erzgebirge region of East Germany was called "Year-end Winged Figure" in the official GDR jargon. And now I will give you my verse of that time, so that you will also have something to laugh about:

Deutsche Weihnacht! Deutsche Weihnacht!
Bratendunst aus jeder Bude
Deutsche Weihnacht! Deutsche Weihnacht!
Deutsche Weihnacht—ich bin Jude.

(German Christmas! German Christmas!
The smell of roasting from every kitchen [Bude]
German Christmas! German Christmas!
German Christmas—I'm a Jew. [Jude])

Because, of course, I needed a word to rhyme with "Bude." So, you see, I was not completely de-Jewified after all. Yet three years later I was already writing something like this:

Jetzt singe ich für meine Genossen alle
Das Lied von der verratenen Revolution
Für meine verratenen Genossen singe ich
Und ich singe für meine Genossen Verräter.
Das große Lied vom Verrat singe ich
Und das größere Lied von der Revolution.
Und meine Gitarre stöhnt vor Scham
Und meine Gitarre jauchzt vor Glück
Und meine ungläubigen Lippen beten voller Inbrunst
Zu Mensch, dem Gott all meiner Gläubigkeit.

Ich singe für meinen Genossen Dagobert Biermann
Der ein Rauch ward aus den Schornsteinen
Der von Auschwitz stinkend auferstand
In die viel wechselnden Himmel dieser Erde
Und dessen Asche ewig verstreut ist
Über alle Meere und unter alle Völker
Und der jeglichen Tag neu gemordet wird
Und der jeglichen Tag neu aufersteht im Kampf
Und der auferstanden ist mit seinen Genossen
In meinem rauchigen Gesang . . .

(Now I sing for my comrades all
The song of the betrayed revolution
For my betrayed comrades I sing
And I sing for my comrades the betrayers.
The great song of betrayal I sing
And the greater song of the revolution.
And my guitar moans with shame
And my guitar jumps for joy
And my unbelieving lips pray full of devotion

To human beings, the god of all my belief.
I sing for my comrade Dagobert Biermann
Who became a cloud of smoke from the chimneys
Who rose from the dead, stinking, at Auschwitz,

Into the changing heavens of this earth
And whose ashes are forever strewn
Over all oceans and among all peoples
And who is murdered all over again each day
And who rises again from the dead each day to fight
And who rose from the dead with his comrades
In my smoky song . . .)

And so on. I must sing it for you sometime, Ellen, it was my
mother's favorite song. My father was murdered all over again
each day by his so-called comrades in the Party leadership
who had long since forgotten what they once set out to do
and what so many courageous people gave their lives for. Because I am a communist, I have not been a Communist for a
long time now.

That is the deep rupture which Georg Büchner knew. In
Hyperion Hölderlin writes: ". . . I can think of no people as divided as the Germans." That brings to mind the Talmudic
counterpart: What can be more whole than a divided heart?

But the heart of the vast majority of Germans isn't divided at
all, it's only their country that was. And even now, after "*Wie-
dervereinigung*"—reunification—the divide is still growing
deeper. The word should actually be written without the
"e"—"*Widervereinigung*"—not "re"-unification, but rather
"counter"-unification, or unification against one's will. There
was a time when I always thought the division of our fatherland
was at least a small punishment for the great crime committed
by the Germans against the Jewish people. Today I sometimes
spitefully think that the Germans are only now experiencing
the true punishment: the estranged brothers are now forced to
live under one roof. Envy, avarice, greed, malevolence.

You see, dear Ellen, I cannot really give you anything on
the subject of Jews, since, after all, I'm a goy, everything I try
to do turns into German. But show this letter to your British
friend before you put it away. If she wants to print anything
from it for her American readers, tell her to go ahead.

Oh, You're Jewish? That's Okay

by Yael Grözinger

"Things won't be normal between Germans and Jews until a German can call a Jew an asshole if he feels like it." This is the answer one non-Jewish television journalist gave in response to the complaint of young Jews: "Why are Jews so special? Every time a Jew clears his throat, it makes the news—how come?" Jewish life is not a normal part of everyday life in Germany. Announcements for upcoming piano concerts or exhibition openings will say "the Jewish pianist from Riga" or "the artist is the daughter of a Jewish merchant family." As if that were somehow a big deal. Yet at the same time we find that Jews are discovering many new ways of defining Jewish life for themselves. What follows is a description of some of my own personal observations. I do not claim that they paint a representative picture of Jewish society as a whole, but they should provide an idea of some of the Jewish institutions that exist here and the environment in which young Jews interact.

Most young Jews go to German public schools. Berlin is the only place with a private Jewish high school, which opened recently, but only some of the students and teachers are Jewish. Several of the larger communities have Jewish kindergartens and elementary schools, however. If children receive religious instruction at all, for the majority it is outside school, and even then it is only available to children who live in the cities. However, the Jewish communities do have quite a lot to offer their young people in the way of facilities and activities, such as youth centers, dance, music and discussion groups, where they can get together in their free time to hang out or organize events. Occasionally they have Hanukkah discos or Purim parties. In other words, young people do have opportunities to build up a circle of Jewish friends in addition to their non-Jewish friends from school.

The Central Welfare Office, the most important Jewish social service organization in Germany, organizes vacation camps that combine recreation and learning in Germany and abroad, usually in Israel or in the small German town of Sobernheim. The German Union of Jewish Students also organizes courses for people aged 18 and over, which include trips abroad. The subjects covered revolve around Israeli politics, Judaism in the media, the history of the Jews; a recent study trip, for example, was a four-day seminar in Istanbul on the subject of Turkish Jews.

These events help to cultivate a sense of community awareness among the young people by bringing together Jews from communities all over Germany. One of the side-benefits of these gatherings is their function as a meeting place for Jewish singles who are looking for a marriage partner, although, unfortunately, the choice is not all that great—there are simply not enough Jews around . . . Maybe that is also the main reason why the controversial subject of "mixed marriages" is becoming such a major issue.

It may come as a surprise that, within Germany, it is possible to lead a life embedded almost entirely in Jewish society. There's something for everyone. Women in their thirties have the option of joining the WIZO-Aviv (Women's International Zionist Organization), and when they are older, the WIZO. However, it is not all that easy to feel comfortable in this organization if your financial resources are limited. Senior citizens have their clubs where they meet to play cards. There are also B'nai B'rith lodges which are open to both young people and adults, male and female. The B'nai B'rith presents a solid, middle-class image and likes to invite illustrious speakers to its meetings. Every local group has its own hierarchy, with a chairperson, a vice-chairperson, a treasurer, etc. There are a whole lot of little clubs for the sake of variety—and for the sake of more chairpersons, vice-chairpersons, treasurers, etc.

A difficult problem that has emerged in recent years is the integration of new Russian immigrants. The families who have lived here for a long time have formed closed cliques of people who have known each other since childhood and have been through kindergarten and school together. So, new members of the community have a hard time making contacts. This is true of all age-groups. Distrust, arrogance and above all insecurity play a major role. The relationship between Jews in this country is ambivalent. The following story, which took place at Frankfurt University, is entirely typical:

There is one hour to go before an oral exam. The teaching assistant quickly sums up some of the main points that will come up in the exam. The atmosphere is amiable and jocular. As he bends forward to make a point about something, a chain with a gold pendant slips out from under his shirt collar. "What's that?" one student asks. The TA answers in a lecturing tone: "That's a *chai*, a Hebrew character that means life!" The student is pleased—the moment has come for him to reach inside his own collar. He, too, is wearing a pendant around his neck, and now the TA sees it, too. Two Jews have found each other. A bridge has suddenly formed between them. They are allies. The other students are watching these two as if they came from another planet. Although the two are bursting with curiosity, they try not to show it, they keep it between them, a matter between two Jews, with knowing looks and the inevitable question as to the other's last name. The student wonders: Do I know his family? Wasn't there a wedding, or a bar mitzvah for his younger brother last year? They do not ask why they haven't met in the Jewish community yet; or where the other one lives—or whether he is even a Frankfurt Jew. If he comes from Cologne or Munich, for example, then it's quite possible that they have never heard of

118

each other. In that case, all one has to do is ask one's parents or another Jew—someone is bound to know something. It's always that way.

Certain that they will soon discover each other's life story, they go home.

One week later, the student runs into the TA on the "Fressgass" at one of Frankfurt's street festivals (where one always meets a lot of Jews out for a stroll). The spontaneous feeling of being allies that they had at the university is now gone. It has given way to the phenomenon of "Jewish-Jewish intertrust," a mixture of interest, courtesy, mistrust, insecurity, staking out territory and grinning.

Each of the two has already found out everything he wanted to know about the other. As if they'd known each other all their lives. Jews do not appear out of the blue. Everybody knows everybody else in a village. Now these two can speak to each other more openly. But they had definitely wanted to avoid asking each other questions in front of the non-Jewish students. The non-Jews should not get the idea that there was some kind of Jewish conspiracy going on here.

Many Jews speak in terms of "the Germans" and "us Jews" to set themselves off. They are apparently unaware—or they don't care—that this does not exactly help to close the culture gap between Jews and non-Jews. As is most likely the case in all social groups around the world, they are proud of the group to which they belong, and this tends to create an even greater social distance between them and their environment. It is not a matter of giving up one's identity but of practicing the same kind of tolerance that one expects of others.

Religion does not play a very big role in the lives of most young Jews. If you ask a teenager what Judaism essentially means to him, he will tell you: "The tradition, the history, the sense of belonging." Hardly anyone will say: "The religion and the culture." The fact that religious devotion is not what counts most can be gathered from the sumptuous festivities that take place on the occasion of a bar mitzvah or a wedding.

Anyone who can afford it (or is willing to go into debt) tries to make it the best ever at the most expensive hotel. An event of paramount social importance! True, for the high holidays everyone comes together in the synagogue, but more out of a sense of tradition than to pray.

Completely in line with tradition, people still assign a great deal of importance to education. "My son the doctor" is not just a joke about proud Yiddish mamas. It is a fact that a disproportionate number of Jews study medicine, law and economics.

If you ask a Jew whether he keeps kosher, he is quite likely to answer: "Sometimes." A contradiction in itself. There is no certified kosher food to be had in a normal German supermarket. In many of the larger cities, there is a little Jewish store tucked away somewhere that has to provide for the whole community. But hardly anyone is willing or able to go to all the extra trouble. So, while many people may not eat pork—except perhaps in sausages or maybe even as ham—they happily eat shrimp and meat in a cream sauce.

In terms of culture, there is quite a bit going on right now among Jewish students and the younger generation, especially in Frankfurt.

Up to now, the American chapel on the U.S. army complex has given the followers of a more liberal practice of Judaism an alternative to the Orthodox religious service at the main synagogue. Now that the Americans are going home, a small group of Frankfurt Jews has organized an alternative community. The meaning of the religious act is explained here in German instead of Hebrew and thus attracts those who would like to do more to preserve their Jewish identity, but who do not know enough about their religion to understand all of the rituals.

During the Purim season in 1994, students performed an old Purim play as one of the events commemorating the 1200th anniversary of the City of Frankfurt, in the framework of a congress on the history of Jews in Frankfurt. It was a play

120

that had been banned by the Jewish Community in 1708 because it was considered obscene. Jewish and non-Jewish students and young people collaborated on this performance of a Yiddish play with Yiddish music, and the event attracted a big audience.

There are a small number of Jewish print media. Recently, the Frankfurt student newspaper *Chuzpe* has been gaining in popularity among young people. It has a circulation of 1,000 and reaches quite a few Jewish communities and libraries, students and adults, Jews and non-Jews. This publication runs articles about politics, is satirical and entertaining in parts, and is also a forum for the experiments and opinions of a mixed audience and the regional chapter of the German Union of Jewish Students. One of its non-partisan political campaigns was the following appeal launched to coincide with the local elections in the State of Hesse in 1993: "Go vote! Your vote counts: Vote for anything you think is right, but not the extreme right!" The campaign was supported by prominent figures in Hesse and Germany as a whole, leading philosophers such as Jürgen Habermas, for example, Ignatz Bubis, chairman of the Central Council of Jews in Germany, actors, athletes, writers, disco owners and many more. In the newspaper and on the radio, pitches were made against giving up on politics and the system and in favor of a democratic consciousness. The activists (myself included) distributed leaflets with the "Go vote!" slogan on it in Frankfurt's main shopping district, and so there was a lot of direct feedback from passersby. At one point, two of us were suddenly surrounded by about ten people who were screaming, spitting at us, baring their hatred. Their anger was not directed against the appeal but against the initiators—the Jewish students. Here are some of the things they actually said, and I quote: "You Jews should finally pay for what you've done to us over the past 2,000 years!"; "The media are crawling with Jews!"; "Jews are whipping up hatred against the nationalist parties—the Jews are the real right-wing extremists!"; "The Jew is sucking us

Germans dry"; "Why don't you go back to Israel?"; "You should look after the Palestinians instead!"; "If you were working for me, Jewish student, you'd soon change your tune!" Of course, there were also positive remarks, but this experience was very typical of the mood at that time.

Jewish students were also among those who called for demonstrations against the attacks on foreigners by right-wing radicals. During the Gulf war, many of them showed up at large demonstrations to show their solidarity with the United States, the Allies and Israel. Many of these demonstrations, organized by German so-called "peace groups" and by students from schools and colleges, were very anti-American. On the whole, a lot of Germans tend to sympathize more with the "oppressed" Palestinians and Arabs in general than they do with the Israelis. The threat to Israel at the time of Gulf War was not very high on the agenda. I was going to a regular high school in a small town at the time. When students and teachers at my school went out to demonstrate, I was afraid that it would turn out to be a march with anti-American slogans. In the end, I joined forces with a grand total of three other people who were in favor of the Allied intervention. Our poster said: "War is bad but Saddam is worse!" We were put down and bitterly attacked for it, even by teachers. We were warmongers, they said. Afraid of severe reprisals, we decided not to take part in the demonstration. Instead, children who were only 11 years old, and understood even less about politics than most of the students in the upper grades, went along with the demonstrators, carrying the usual signs "No blood for oil!" People were more afraid of what might happen to their ecological environment if Saddam carried out his threat to ignite the oil fields than they were of what might happen to the Israelis if he launched a military attack. For that matter, peace marches for ex-Yugoslavia have never drawn the same masses that those for the Gulf did, and neighboring Yugoslavia is much closer to home for the Germans than the Middle East.

Israel and the United States, however, were a thorn in people's sides.

The Jews, and not just Israel and its politics, are a favorite topic of discussion and arouse curiosity, both in the media and among drinking buddies in the local bars. I, too, am one of the many who have been invited in their capacity as a Jew to take part in discussions on the radio, in newspapers or on television. As a "real-live Jew" (many people have never knowingly seen one), each of us then tries to show that we are not the "reproachful victims" which many German non-Jews consider Jews to be. Many are surprised to find out that a Jew is just an ordinary person. It seems that a lot of people are not neutral, but have either a "negative image" or a "positive image" of Jews. Here are a few personal experiences of my own to show what I mean:

It is December 23 and I am standing in the checkout line at the supermarket. There is a full grocery cart in front of me. A pink Christmas goose is peeking out. The woman with the cart still remembers me from when I was in kindergarten. She is trying to figure out what these poor Jews must do with themselves at Christmas time. So she asks me, "Are you going home to Israel over the holidays?" As if I were not at home in Germany.

A fellow student at the university fancies young Jewish women. One morning during the lecture I feel someone's warm breath in my ear: "Bohker Toohf." That was Bavarian Hebrew for "Good morning." He wants to know when "Shanukka" is and what subway will take him to the synagogue.

A neighbor asks in passing, "Do you happen to know a Samuel Perlmann?" I say, "No." One week later the same neighbor says, "These speculators in Frankfurt with their exorbitant rents—that guy Silberberg is one of them!" Then, "You're Jewish, aren't you?" He is quite proud of himself for having guessed. Since then I have been asked to give an opinion on everything from Biblical sayings to the peace pro-

cess. It is assumed that I know intimately every Jewish person-
ality in the country and can discuss their comings and goings.
How do I like "that Michel Friedman" (a colorful Jewish
politician), and "How much power does Bubis really have?
Can he order all of the Jews to go to Israel now?"

It also helps to know when the musician Giora Feidman
will be back in town, what is kabbalistic about the film *The
Seventh Seal*, and also what the opening hours of the Jewish
Museum are.

When are questions good and when are they irritating?

You cannot necessarily tell that I am Jewish from the way I
look. But if I identify myself as such, some people say, "How
interesting." Others console me with the words, "Oh, that's
okay." Both reactions show in their own way how Jews are
often forced into playing a certain role. One role is meant in a
positive way and the other is meant to be bad. Anti-Semitism
and philo-Semitism are two sides of the same coin.

When I was 12 years old, a bunch of boys in their early
teens had a crush on me; then, when nothing came of it, their
love turned into hate. A rotten egg hit my door, a flaming pile
of dog-turds was left smoldering on my doormat, and one day
the same boys shouted "*Juden raus!*" (Jews get out!)

Anti-Semitism at school was usually couched in criticism of
Israel: "You're oppressing the Arabs. You're just like the
Nazis!" And I should defend myself? As a German Jew, a Jewish German or a Jew in Germany—as they say—all I can do is
try to inform; if anyone has any explaining to do, it should be
the Israeli politicians, not me.

My name is Yael, but my ethics teacher at school would call
me "Israel" just to provoke me. Once, when I skipped class,
he told me "Go back to Israel, we don't want you here!"

Many people make a point of acting pro-Jewish because
they are afraid of looking anti-Jewish. Does their guilty conscience make philo-Semites out of them?

Some people like to point out that they come from a family
that was involved in the resistance during the Third Reich.

124

"Everyone had a Jew in the cellar." They defend themselves without having been accused of anything. A guilty conscience?

When I was eight years old, I went to a Sunday School class with my girlfriends. We were taught that "God loves all Christians!" But I wanted God to love me, too. The teacher consoled me, sat me on her lap, stroked my head and gave me books to take home. She did not do that with her little Christian lambs. Which shows just how early you can become a professional Jew.

There are radical anti-Semites and vehement philo-Semites. There is a negative image of the "Jew" and a positive image of the "Jew." As long as people still need any kind of image of the Jew, a Jew will remain something strange and exotic. I think we should be charging admission.

Plea for an Inwardly Directed German Nationalism

by Michael Wolffsohn

What could be more natural than to look at the realities of democratic reality in Germany and describe them as reality, in spite of the present and Nazi history? Because exactly that—no more and no less—is what I have attempted to do in my work as a scholar and journalist. Although I have been wearing glasses ever since my formative political years, I have never seen German-Jewish reality through ideologically tinted glasses. That is not because of anything I have done; it is the result of my biography. My own personal experience of contemporary history has engendered in me a distinctly counter-historical form of German-Jewish patriotism in a quite natural and highly non-ideological manner; it has shaped the process in which my German and Jewish roots are equally embedded, my identity. My very own personal microcosm has always been a part of the political macrocosm of the times, and this is how a living fossil emerged, a German-Jewish patriot—in other words, me. Why did that happen, and how?

Like every other human being, I was born—*natus sum*, in Latin. *Natus sum*—into a nation. The word "nation" (which has any number of negative historical connotations, in Germany and elsewhere, and is embarrassing, even irritating, for some), the word "nation" points to the plain and simple fact, the natural (in the literal sense) fact that we are born not only into our own little family but at the same time into a larger community. And this larger community into which we are born is the nation to which we belong.

Was I born into one nation? My parents and grandparents came from Germany and were living in Tel Aviv ("Palestine" at that time, Israel today) when I was born in 1947. In other words, my father's country was actually Germany. And German was also my native language, since my parents' and grandparents' Hebrew was halting at best, and still is. Even before I came to Germany as a seven year-old in 1954, German was my native language, even in Israel, and Germany was my father's native country. Not only from an objective point of view, but also spiritually. Like many other emigrés, especially German emigrés, my parents and grandparents always remained strangers in their new Israeli home.

Where do I belong? Where are my roots? Where does my future lie? What am I? An Israeli? A Jew? Only an Israeli? Only a German? Only a Jew? Every human being has an identity. Some people do not have to seek it out, others never find it. I had to search for it and find it, because mine was also determined by different places and thus imbued with different meanings. These questions were answered for me when I moved from Germany to Israel and lived there from 1967 to 1970. What did I have to do? I had to listen to my inner voice. Lessons I had gleaned from national, collective history were empty phrases that were useless to me in attempting to determine where I belonged and what path I should take. I had to rely instead on my inner senses, triggered by external occasions and events. And what did I find out? That I unquestionably had Jewish inner feelings. More cultural than purely religious in nature, but religious as well. My national feelings, on the other hand, were stronger in relation to Germany than they were to Israel, in spite of the alleged lessons to be learned from German-Jewish history. No, I was not indifferent to Israel and the Israelis, and never have been, but I had stronger vibrations when it came to Germany and the Germans. I was happier when I heard good things about Germany, and I was more aggravated when I heard aggravating things about Germany. I found Golda Meir fascinating, but the controversies surrounding Willy Brandt's *Ostpolitik* at the time were even more riveting. Israel and the PLO were topics which moved me. But the post-1968 student protest movement was even more exciting. Israel had good writers back then, too. I could read them. But I wanted to read more and more German writers, and always came back to them. The Israeli *Haaretz* was already an excellent newspaper in those days, not as overbearing as most German daily newspapers. But I still had withdrawal symptoms if there were no German daily newspapers around. And without the weekly irritation of *Der Spiegel*,★ the irritation was only half as irritating. The Tel Aviv theater was pretty good and politically less abrasive than the Berlin Schaubühne am Halleschen Ufer. But without the dry humor of the Schaubühne, theater was not really theater. And even the Israel Philharmonic Orchestra, as good as it was, could not take the place of the Berlin Philharmonic. For me, the nation was a primary "communicative community," to use Karl W. Deutsch's words. Applied social sciences. In addition to the theory, I now also had the practice, my own experience, to back it up.

My feeling was, the move to Israel was a kind of transplantation, Germany was my native soil, my nature—my nation.

Nature and nation. Both terms go back to the Latin *natus sum*, to birth and thus to life as such.

Concepts do not come into being by chance. They describe realities. Words not only reflect external realities, but also the internal realities of the soul. The concepts of nation, patriotism, fatherland and mother tongue reflect inner realities that are common to all human beings, and not just in their German equivalents. We find the same conceptual pattern in other languages as well, or at least in the ones I know—in English and French, in Italian and in Spanish, and also in Hebrew. In Hebrew, *moledet* is the word for nation. The word *moledet* also refers to birth and thus to father and mother, and thus, in the final instance, to love.

So, it is quite natural for a human being to love his fatherland and his mother tongue, to be a patriot in other words, because he has more than his biological life to thank them for. The national feeling is a natural feeling, a matter of course, because the words *to love* and *to live* have a common root in German and thus also a common spiritual reality.

In other words, the kind of patriotism I am talking about here is nationalism in the very literal sense of the word (*natus sum*). And this nationalism is something quite natural. But—it is a form of nationalism which is *inwardly* directed, a reflection of something on the inside, within the soul. It is not aimed at anything or anyone, it is not pointed outward, much less *against* anything on the outside.

Patriotism means identifying with what is worth loving and living for in a country, or striving to make that country worth loving and living in because it is one's own country. Without this inwardly oriented nationalism, without this kind of patriotism, a nation is denaturalized. It is injured. And Germany is an "injured nation." Elisabeth Noelle-Neumann, a leading opinion pollster, put it in these typically clear terms and backed up the idea with empirical data in a highly readable book. Germany is a nation which has been injured because of German history. Germany is still licking the wounds that it inflicted upon itself—and, in the process, on others as well. I am deliberately putting this in seemingly redundant terms: If Germany does not find its way back to a natural, inwardly oriented form of nationalism, if it does not find itself, it will not find *inner* peace. But if you do not find inner peace, you cannot secure or instill enduring peace on the *outside*.

Of course, Germany does not need me to find either inner peace or peace with others. But if there is anything which I as an individual can contribute to a community, my community, my nation, it would be this constant plea for an inner sense of nationalism among Germans. Given my biography, I am above all suspicion and can ask the Germans to strive for an inner sense of nationalism without arousing suspicion. For their own sake and the sake of their environment.

It is not ironic, and also not grotesque, but if anything, tragic and a result of German history that not only can a Jew make such a plea today but almost only a Jew can do it without making himself suspect. And for the time being I am the one who must do this so that every German will soon be able to do it for himself and his environment. This is the commandment under which I have come forward as an individual—based on my biography. I was born with it. It was not through any achievement of my own. A refusal to do so would have been like running away.

There are many who contend that the German-Jewish patriot Wolffsohn is being paraded as an alibi. A token Jew, an alibi Jew in the wake of the deplorable acts of violence against foreigners in Rostock and Sachsenhausen, in Mölln and Solingen, Lübeck and Magdeburg. And some may also have thought this was the case when I gave the keynote address celebrating the tenth anniversary of Chancellor Kohl's term in office on October 2, 1992. And my reply? There were times in Germany when chancellors, leaders and Führers did not put Jews on a public platform, but instead had them picked up, taken away and murdered. Who, by the same token, would have thought in 1945 that any German Jew could have been willing, for his part, to hold the keynote address for the first chancellor in a Germany reunited in freedom, regardless of the political party to which the chancellor belonged?

When the Christian-Socialist Party in Munich asked me in 1992 to stand for the office of cultural administrator in Germany's largest municipality (not town), it showed once more that things had changed, what had changed and how much had changed in Germany—and changed for the better. It was on November 9 of that year that I was called upon to accept the office. Is there any more portentous date to symbolize the change which has taken place? I know very well: On November 9, 1938, my maternal grandfather was carried off to Dachau by the SA. "But I was a Royal Bavarian uhlan in World War I," my grandfather had told the SA thugs. The effect was immediate: They beat him over the head with a rubber truncheon.

In October 1992, I received the "Pro Humanitate" medal awarded by the West-Ost-Kulturwerk, an organization which is actively involved in the integration of ethnic Germans who have come to Germany from eastern Europe and supports the cause of those who were driven out of their homelands behind the then Iron Curtain. But it faces this task in a spirit of reconciliation with Poles and Czechs, without denying German guilt, bridging the abyss, seeking dialogue (without reproaches).

There are certainly many others who also deserved a medal for humanity, "Pro Humanitate." Jews as well as non-Jews, for humanity is not the prerogative of one nation or religion. But neither is inhumanity.

What is more, the West-Ost-Kulturwerk awarded me the "Pro Humanitate" medal long before the crimes in Rostock, Sachsenhausen, Mölln and other places were committed. So there can be no question of an alibi here. Nor does the overwhelming majority of Germans in the West or the East need an alibi. The fact is, surveys have shown that 86 percent of the Germans condemned the infamous acts committed in Rostock, Sachsenhausen and the like. That is almost exactly the same percentage of people who, as we have known for years, are firmly in favor of democracy and tolerance, and reject anti-Semitism and xenophobia. In other words, Germany is healthy at heart, so to speak. Two percent condone shameful acts of this kind. That is not much but still a lot. Too many. After all, two percent of the German population means roughly 1.5 million people. But, even so, we are talking about two percent and not 98 percent. This is exactly where we see the problem of our German present. And what is the problem? That a minority is able to dictate what happens to the overwhelming majority, is able to set the political agenda. Politics is actually a steering process. For the ancient Romans, the politician was a *gubernator*, a helmsman: the man (at that time, the prerogative of men), the man who guided, steered and thus ruled the ship of state. Politicians who increasingly shift the decision-making process "onto the street" through non-parliamentary opposition, demonstrations in other words, merely weaken our institutions. They merely highlight their own lack of justification—and then are surprised when people get "fed up" with politics, their parties and the government. By their own actions, they make the sea on which the ship of state sails ever choppier and have problems steering the ship as a result.

The political fringe groups are eating their way into the heart of our commonality, which is actually healthy to the core. A form of nationalism which is directed outward and against others, and is dangerous for that reason, is gaining ground. It is not the inwardly directed nationalism, the inwardly oriented patriotism I was talking about in the beginning. This form of nationalism that is turned against others is gaining ground in Germany and in other countries as well. Of course, we cannot use the stupidity and dangerous sentiments of others as an alibi for ourselves. We are the ones who must first come to terms with those among us who are misguided, insane, misleading and criminal. These people call themselves German patriots, and many of them shout "Heil Hitler!" But anyone who is still yelling "Heil Hitler!" today, or is doing so again, does not love Germany; does not want love and life, which is to say, true patriotism for Germans and Germany, but hatred and death for Germany and the environment. Adolf Hitler was responsible not only for the deaths of six million Jews and 45 million people of other ethnic groups. Adolf Hitler also had the deaths of five million Germans on his conscience. His policies left Germany devastated in 1945, morally contemptible, and the Germans deeply afflicted in their natural feeling of being a nation. Hitler despised the Germans. The so-called "scorched earth" directive of March 19, 1945 proves it. With this directive, Hitler condemned Germany and its people to death, as Sebastian Haffner

132

pointed out in his superb book *Anmerkungen zu Hitler* (Notes on Hitler). Germany and the Germans were supposed to go under, to die. Germany, go to hell! That was the essence of the command Hitler gave. And now these cocky would-be tough guys are raising their outstretched arms once again to give the Hitler salute. The foreigners are supposed to get out and the Jews, too, they howl. Quite aside from the moral dimension, which is actually self-evident: Do these howlers crying out *"Deutschland"* know that Germany cannot survive without exports, which is to say, without foreign countries and foreigners, and would soon become destitute at best? They are pulling the rug out from under their own feet.

As a Jew, of course, I am especially affected by this. But it is not primarily the problem of the Jews, it is the problem of the non-Jews. After 1945, the Germans in the western part of Germany built up a Germany which, for the first time, truly flourished as a free and just society. Since October 3, 1990, this Germany now also has the potential to flourish in unity, in other words in "unity, justice and freedom." Germans who want to trample out this free and just German state do not love Germany, they are not nationalists because they destroy the nation, that which is natural, life and love. The revamped right-wing extremism is a recipe for collective suicide for Germany and the Germans. To paraphrase Wilhelm Busch (and deliberately unacademically), one could say this about Germans who, for whatever reason, join the right-wing extremists: "Only the stupidest of calves pick their own butchers."

In spite of and because of the 85 percent who believe in democracy in Germany: As far as I am concerned, the title and contents of my book *Keine Angst vor Deutschland!* (Have no fear of Germany!), originally published in 1990 and followed by an expanded edition in 1992, still hold true. But I am deeply concerned nonetheless. Not only for Germany, but for Europe as well: In many East European countries, the Communists made the strongest showing in free elections.

The PDS—the Party of Democratic Socialism (formerly the Communist party which ruled East Germany)—has reason to rejoice. In East Berlin, it got about 30 percent of the votes in the local elections in 1992, and in the new German states as a whole it can draw on about 10 percent of voters. That is what the surveys tell us.

More recent impressions and experiences in my immediate environment, at my university (the University of the German Armed Forces in Munich), were also politically shocking and depressing for me in 1992–93. A few representatives of this university (including one of its former presidents) regarded public readings of Hitler texts (even on the occasion of events commemorating the anniversary of the attempt on Hitler's life on July 20, 1945) as an acceptable form of presentation and representation. However, I was encouraged by the sponta-neous expressions of sympathy I received from numerous politicians, journalists, scholars and generals.

For months now, I have had the dubious "honor" of re-ceiving more and more baskets full of hate mail (and more than ever from western Germany, mind you) which can only be described as primitively and rabidly anti-Semitic. A few of my fellow Jews have overreacted to me, too. They consider me (to quote the words of the journalist Ginzel) "more dan-gerous than the skinheads." Since 1988, the *Allgemeine Jüdische Wochenzeitung,*★ the paper for "all" Jews in Germany as the title would have it, has stuck to the instruction once given by Heinz Galinski (the former chairman of the Central Council of Jews in Germany) not to print any articles written by me or to mention my name. So, whenever there were differences of opinion between us (which was of course very often the case), I was referred to "between the lines" like some name-less phantom. Galinski's successor, Ignatz Bubis, has de-nounced me as a follower of the "so-called Republicans," the ultra-right-wing party in Germany. An outrageous accu-sation, even though he had a copy of an ultra-right-wing flyer which read: "And that Jewish swine Wolffsohn will be the first one we blow away." And why? Because as a Professor of History at the Military Academy in Munich, I am supposedly contaminating the minds of the young breed of German officers.

Ignatz Bubis was peeved at my criticism of his election to his present post. The reason for my criticism was that the gray area between business interests and political office is too structurally risky. The Social Democratic Party in Berlin is anything but exemplary, but it did insist that Walter Momper, its one-time frontrunner there, decide between business and politics. Should we Jews be judged by different standards (which now work to our advantage)? I consider that unwise. It can only make trouble. And we cannot afford to provoke it, nor do we want to, whether we are Jews or non-Jews. I know of no other businessman besides Ignatz Bubis who purports to be the moral conscience of the nation.

After Mölln, Bubis (a member of the Free Democratic Party, FDP, which is in the governing coalition with the Christian-Democrats/Christian-Socialists) said: It is now high time to demonstrate against this government. I say that, now more than ever, it is time to start working together with the politicians in the democratic parties for this democratic state. In the meantime, Bubis has changed his position; he now says that he likes the taste of the soup in Germany, he just has something against a hair here or there. I can live with that. And Bubis can live with me and I with him.

More important, however, is that the leadership of Jews in Germany must finally be split up, into a political leadership, on the one hand, and a spiritual leadership, on the other. Up to now, the political dimension has also included the intellectual-spiritual dimension, which shows how German Judaism has been emptied of its religious substance. In the long run, this poses a great internal danger.

We do not have to waste any time talking about the frivolous idea of Jews or non-Jews taking up arms against xenophobic and anti-Semitic criminals. The Jewish journalist

135

Ralph Giordano had this idea. An idea that would ultimately lead to a civil war. It would be a throwback to the Middle Ages—before feuding was prohibited.

True, it is hard to be optimistic when bad things happen at the macro- and micro-levels at the same time. The germ of stupidity and outwardly oriented nationalism has naturally infected Jews as well. I say naturally, because they, too, are only human. And human beings will be human beings. In the fall of 1992, for example, Jews from France came to Rostock looking for trouble, telling themselves and others that Rostock was setting the stage for another Auschwitz, that 1992, like the *Reichskristallnacht** in 1938, was the beginning of the "final solution." Meanwhile, other French Jews were attacking the Paris branch of the Goethe Institute (the German cultural institution), of all things. An institution that is known in Paris and throughout the world for German cultural policy, but certainly not for German chauvinism.

The Jewish answer to Rostock and Sachsenhausen, and to Ravensbrück and Überlingen and Mölln, and so on and so forth, must not take the form of attacks by Jewish thugs on German policemen, Goethe Institutes, anyone or anything else, for that matter. Violence does not lead to non-violence when it is used by Jews. Democracies need forceful arguments, not the use of force.

Any talk about a Fourth Reich is wrong, outrageous and politically damaging because it provokes spiteful reactions. In the Third Reich, the government organized the crimes; today the government is protecting us. Unfortunately it is not always successful. It is also difficult for it to do so because our police has had its teeth drawn for about 20 years. And now (all of a sudden) it is supposed to bite. No, 1995 is not 1938. Rostock, Mölln, Solingen, Lübeck, Magdeburg are not Auschwitz, and they are also not the harbinger of Auschwitz. Nonetheless we must remain wary and bare our teeth. If only to keep the differences between the two periods of history as different as they are. That is the common task of non-Jews

136

and Jews alike. It brings us together, it does not separate us, because it reinforces our natural German inner world, which is inwardly directed and open to the outside—against the unnatural nationalists who are shaky on the inside and hardened to the outside.

From: Michael Wolffsohn, "Um einen Nationalismus von innen bittend" from *Verwirrtes Deutschland?* edition ferenczy bei Bruckmann, Munich 1993

Through Russian Eyes

by Sofia Mill

I've already been living in Germany for two years!

Not as a citizen, nor as a visitor, but as a person called a "quota-refugee." What exactly does the term mean? This is something that not only we, the quota-refugees, are finding hard to figure out—so too are the government officials who have to deal with us.

We quota-refugees are Jews from the ex-Soviet Union. For the most part, we keep trying to guess why Germany has decided to let us in. Some of us believe that Germany is admitting Soviet Jews in order not to pay reparations to Israel; others insist that Germany has decided to restore the genetic heritage which was destroyed by the Nazis and is trying to raise the number of Jews here so that they make up the same percentage of the overall population as they did before the war. Yet, these are just hypotheses, and the fact that we don't know the real reason for our presence vaguely troubles quite a few of us: what if we're being fattened like a Christmas goose?

When my family and I were offered the opportunity to emigrate to Germany three years ago while we were still in the Soviet Union, we grabbed at the straw. Israel was overfilled, the United States was not accepting anyone, and life at home was getting scarier from one day to the next. Now, however, we sometimes ask ourselves how wise we were.

How do ex-Soviet Jews feel in Germany? Before trying to answer this question, I should mention that ex-Soviet Jews have only two things in common: they're all Russian speakers

138

and all of them carry a "red-skinned" Soviet passport. What they lack is a unifying Jewish basis, a Jewish religious identity. This is not and could not be there. How could a Soviet Jew, unless he is over 70 years old, have any roots in Judaism?

Mind you, I'm talking now about those people whose Soviet passports contain the entry "Jew." But in so many of the families that have come here, there is just one "half-Jew" for every four to five non-Jews. So if by inviting Soviet Jews to come here, the German government has in mind to restore its Jewish community, I don't think it has much chance of succeeding.

A Jewish community is naturally the first place a freshly-baked immigrant hastens to show up, especially if he has no relatives or friends in the country. Where else should he go? Of course, to his own, to the Jews! Yet, here it turns out that "a Jew" in Russian and in German mean quite different things. Whereas in Russian, the word "Jew" refers to the person's ethnic heritage, in German this means nothing more than his or her religion. And thanks to the overwhelming success of the Soviet system in bringing up atheist citizens, it is hardly surprising that the immigrant who arrives at the Jewish community center expects to find a club of secular compatriots. But in Germany, a Jewish community is first and foremost a religious organization.

As a rule, a Jew from the ex-Soviet Union is not ready for that. At the beginning, most newcomers go along to community gatherings, either when religious services are held or when community officials are available to see those members who need advice and help. Later, however, when it becomes clear that the community has exhausted its ability to assist, about 80 percent of the immigrants disappear forever or show up perhaps once or twice a year. As it turns out, the communities, especially small ones, cannot help very much, and they can do less and less as the influx of immigrants becomes larger and larger.

Take my community, the Jewish Community of Bochum-

Herne-Recklinghausen; because of the influx of ex-Soviet Jews in the past two years, it has grown twenty-fold! Yet, of all these new community members, only a handful have jobs and are paying church taxes, so it is not too surprising that the joy with which the local "German" Jews at first welcomed the newcomers is now turning into something close to terror.

However, it would be wrong to give the impression that the communities are not trying hard to bring the immigrants together, to foster social contact and establish informal networks, which are direly needed by most of us new immigrants. Even our small and financially limited community holds biweekly German classes for elderly people who are not eligible for state-sponsored language education. Once a week, the elderly members can meet for "a cuppa coffee," once a month, kids and teenagers have a get-together. And, of course, all of the religious holidays are celebrated. Still, most of the newcomers remain outside the orbit of the community.

Once they come to Germany, most immigrants (with only rare exceptions) find themselves under a great deal of stress, caused not just by the upheaval of the emigration itself, but also by their lack of German language skills and their ignorance of German laws and regulations. Of course, it was a lot worse for the early immigrants who had no group experience to fall back on, but even so, everyone has to get through the first stage of filling out a myriad of forms, making contacts and "feeling" his or her way through the unfamiliar western environment.

The second stage, and this applies only to those newcomers who are employable, consists of attending a language school. And this, I believe, is truly the happiest time! No matter that the language lessons are badly organized and one learns a lot less than one could. What is really important is that the "student" feels that a certain progress is being made, and life again makes sense. But sooner or later these courses come to an end. That's when the job-hunting starts—and that's when it becomes clear that finding a job can be like finding a needle in a haystack. Almost 80 percent of the newcomers from the ex-Soviet Union are university graduates, but that doesn't make life any easier for them.

Moreover, a lot of people who were highly qualified "back home" are not even in the running on the job market because Germany does not recognize the university degrees of ex-Soviet teachers and economists. But even for engineers, whose diplomas are recognized, the situation is quite unfavorable: not only is the supply of engineers on the German white-collar labor market generally higher than the demand, but ex-Soviet engineers often cannot compete because their language skills are poor (or non-existent) in German or English—or for that matter, in any other European language.

In most cases, however, the hopeful job-hunters never get as far as being invited by a company for an interview. And what can you do then? About two years ago, this question had a simple answer: return to a continuing education school if you had a recognized degree or diploma, or to a re-training course if you did not, with the state paying all of the expenses, including a scholarship. But last year, the chances of getting to such courses were cut drastically, as the government slashed their financing. Now the situation has slightly improved, and such courses are being offered again, although only those who have worked in Germany for at least one year are eligible for a scholarship. However—whether one's chances to get a job really improve after these courses have been completed is anyone's guess.

One way or another, most of the immigrants are unemployed, and keep "riding the welfare train," as the expression goes. Financially, the situation is bearable, because welfare assistance provides a far higher standard of living than the engineers, for example, could have afforded in the ex-Soviet Union. But socially and psychologically, the situation is very difficult. Most of these highly-trained people worked in the old country not simply to make a living but also because they enjoyed what they were doing. Whether they were engineers, doctors or teachers, they led truly creative lives. And now life has become so empty and meaningless that some of them are beginning to think of going back.

It is hard to say how realistic their plans are. There's a lot of truth in the saying "You can't enter the same river twice." Nevertheless, more and more immigrants are playing with the idea of returning. This may be happening at least in part because for many people, the move to Germany was not a narrow escape (thank God!) from something that they remember with true horror. And then again, perhaps homesickness is quite normal: you live in one country, then move to another, then you realize—no, this isn't where I belong—so you decide to go back. For me, who was socialized in the Soviet Union, it is hard to pass judgement.

Elderly people, too, are having a hard time. The more fortunate ones managed to keep some rudiments of Yiddish alive over the years, so they do not suffer so much from language isolation and can take care of their everyday problems. But almost none of the elderly have much contact with the "natives," and the Russian-speaking population is still not big enough to supply an adequate social infrastructure. What is more, it has become clear that a typical ex-Soviet retiree finds it exceedingly hard to adjust to the "easy" life in the West. Where he or she came from in the ex-Soviet Union, a normal day was taken up by small battles: running from place to place in search of food, standing in long lines at a store to buy what little there was, or at a savings bank to draw a pension. Come the evening, and the tired pensioner could at least boast about the small victories won that day.

Here in Germany, the fighting instinct of an ex-Soviet person has no outlet. And this is very hard for many to accept. So some of them, especially the more active, are beginning to try to get themselves involved in Jewish community politics and are looking for a role in the leadership. It is still difficult to predict how successful their attempts will be because the present "German" leadership is resisting as hard as it can, insisting

142

that to represent a Jewish community at the various levels of German society, a person must, at the very least, speak German well, and be familiar with the German system and its bureaucracy. But I have no doubt that the next elections of the community leadership will see some ex-Soviet Jews entering their ranks, although I am not sure whether the other community members will necessarily benefit from it.

Faces and Places—Speaking Out in Images

Photographs by Todd Weinstein

Berlin   Cemetery memorial

144

Cologne   Kids at kindergarten

Cologne   A kindergarten portrait

Berlin   A Russian immigrant learning to sing

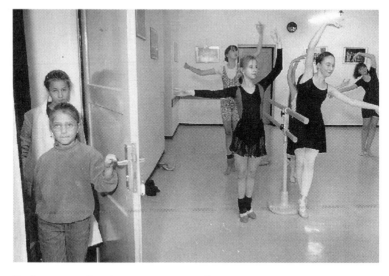

Berlin   Russian immigrants on their toes

146

Berlin   The Community Center café

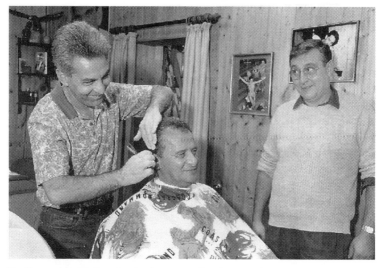

Berlin   A Russian barber at work (observed by Peter Ambros)

Munich   A Sukkot blessing

148

Munich   A distinguished senior citizen

Munich   Aging gracefully

Berlin   "Still in business"

Berlin   Hand over voice (Yiddish singer Jalda Rebling)

150

Frankfurt The Westend Synagogue—loiterers not welcome

Frankfurt The Westend Synagogue—newly renovated interior

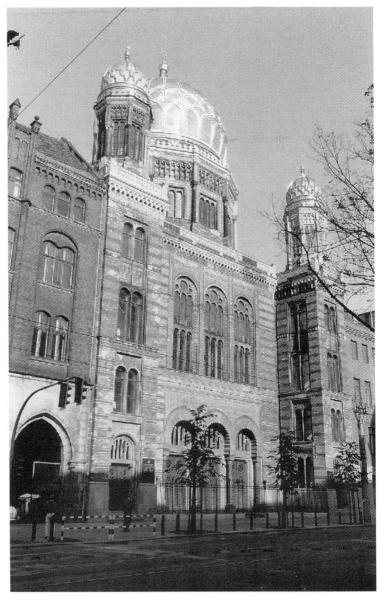

Berlin   The New Synagogue in former East Berlin

Cologne   A synagogue from without

Worms   A synagogue from within

Worms   Polite reminder at the synagogue

Munich   Reflections of son and grandson in a gravestone

154

Speyer   The 12th century ritual bath (*mikveh*)

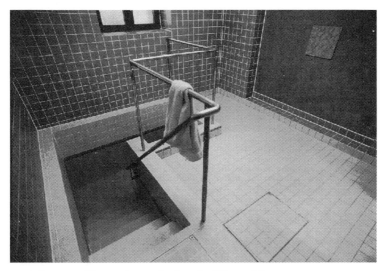

Frankfurt   The modern *mikveh* at the Westend Synagogue

Frankfurt   Mr. Heller's kosher shop

Frankfurt   Mr. Heller at work

Berlin   Kosher shop belonging to Adass Yisroel

Berlin   Through the shop window

Frankfurt   Breaking the fast after Yom Kippur

Berlin   A Sabbath luncheon

Berlin   The Community Center library

Berlin   Heavy security in front of the Community Center

Berlin   Past the tanks and through the doors . . .

Berlin   Activity board at the Berlin-Mitte Community Center

Berlin   Pocked wall, gleaming notice

Munich   A corner of the Jewish Museum

162

Frankfurt   Bird's-eye view at the Jewish Museum annex

Buchenwald   Waiting to get into the concentration camp site

Buchenwald   Hearing about the way it was

164

German Jewry
Squawking at the Approach
of Danger

by Rafael Seligmann

Auschwitz itself was unable to put an end to German-Jewish history; but the way Germans and Jews deal with it may be more successful.

Germans and Jews! Despite 1,600 years of common history, the overwhelming majority of Germans today still do not consider Jews to be Germans, even if they come from families who have lived in Germany centuries longer than their own "German" forebears.

Jews in post-Auschwitz Germany need a thick skin in order to survive. They are supposed to ignore the undercurrent of German anti-Semitism—which, after all, is represented by a share of the population ranging anywhere from 22 percent (Germans who would "prefer not to have any Jewish neighbors") to 39 percent (Germans who think that the Jews "are exploiting the Holocaust for their own ends").

Jews in Germany who are "smart" try to blend in with the indifferent masses and avoid falling into the clutches of the philo-Semites, in other words, those who think that Jews are "better human beings."

A few words should be said about the philo-Semitic attitude. On the face of it, there is nothing wrong with having a good opinion of someone. In practice, however, setting one group off, even in a positive way, amounts to a form of discrimination against other groups in the population. Positive and negative discrimination thus become a function of prejudice rather than objective merit. Philo-Semites claim to believe that Jews per se are morally superior to Germans. The reason for this is the past—Auschwitz, in other words. Because six million Jews were slaughtered in the name of Germany, a highly articulate minority of Germans today feel guilty. They believe, or at least claim to believe, that through suffering, Jews have risen to great heights on the moral scale. On the other hand, the German people as a whole, including not a few fathers, uncles and other members of the immediate family, was plunged "by Hitler" into profound guilt, and must bear the "collective shame" of it, even today—it is interesting to note that hardly anyone speaks of "responsibility" or even of "collective responsibility."

There is a reverse side to this attitude, which many Jews do not want to see until they are directly affected by it. Since it is clear for philo-Semites that the Jews are morally superior, at least since Auschwitz, they are under an obligation to live up to the standards that go with it—no matter what that takes! The Jews should be "good Christians," they must always turn the other cheek. This is also why self-ordained friends of the Jews expect the Israelis to rigorously practice a superior morality. This was quite easy to do until 1967, when Israel found itself confronted by the overwhelming forces of the Arab world who, moreover, vociferously proclaimed that they would "drive the Jews into the sea."

After the Six Day War, Israel itself became an occupying force. There were also times when Israeli soldiers shot at Arab women and children. The philo-Semites were all up in arms. Hadn't the Jews learned anything from Auschwitz and Dachau?

Philo-Semites long for the morally immaculate Jew. They have a craving to wallow in their own guilt in the distorted image of his moral purity.

Everywhere in the world there are and always have been anti-Semites and philo-Semites. But the special German breed of hostility to Jews led to Auschwitz. The Nazi genocide committed against the Jews also forms a major part of the

German philo-Semites' masochistic pleasure. Auschwitz alone, however, is not enough by any means to explain the specific phenomenon of so-called German philo-Semitism. In order to understand the relationship between Germans and Jews, one has to know something about meshuggene German-Jewish history.

Jews have been living in Germany since the fourth century. Thus, Germany has an uninterrupted line of Jewish history that is more than 1,600 years old—in spite of the fact that Germany, in its modern form as a state, has only existed for just over 120 years.

Because of its continuity, Jewish history in Germany is one of the oldest to bind the Jews with any country on earth—the Jewish community in Zion was never blessed with more than a few centuries of survival.

Germany's long Jewish history was one of the reasons for German-Jewish patriotism.

Over the centuries, the German Jews felt an ever stronger affinity with their German homeland. In spite of anti-Semitism and discrimination, in spite of being crowded into ghettos and in spite of the repeatedly erupting pogroms—things were no better any place else, maybe even worse, and in Germany at least, Jews had something to call their own, their own familiar ghetto and their own familiar German language. Even those Jews who were driven out of Germany or left the country of their own accord took part of their homeland with them: the German language. Yiddish, the idiom of millions of Jews in eastern Europe and later even in the New World, is rooted in Middle High German.

When the Enlightenment began to spread throughout Germany in the wake of the French Revolution, an avant-garde of emancipation soon emerged among the Jews as well. Moses Mendelssohn and the ladies of the Berlin salons, such as Rachel Varnhagen von Este, paved the way for this development. The broad masses were not granted *formal* equal rights until the founding of the German Reich in 1871. *Real* emancipation, however, was never achieved by the Jews in Imperial Germany at any time.

Jews were not allowed to hold any high public offices or officer commissions, which were the ego-substitutes of Prussian male elitism. Jews were also barred from the craft trades, heavy industry and many areas of higher education.

In spite of this social discrimination and an omnipresent latent anti-Semitism, the German Jews showed the goyim what kind of potency was dormant in them. Within a few short decades, the Jews who had been banished to the ghetto for centuries conquered leading positions in German culture—in literature, music, painting, in theater, in journalism, in the sciences, in those political parties to which Jews were admitted, in publishing and in business, especially in the textile sector. The Jews, never more than 0.7 percent of the German population, ran rings around their Christian counterparts. They showed 99 percent of the Germans that the culture and intelligence of the people of *"Dichter und Denker"* (poets and philosophers) could not be all that great if Jews accounted for one-fourth of the German Nobel prize-winners, for example, while Jewish authors set the tone and broke decisive new paths in literature and journalism.

As a consequence, anti-Semitism unexpectedly took on new strength, fuelled by envy: Many German intellectuals and merchants saw themselves being outdone by their Jewish competitors, and needed an explanation. But the usefulness of the anti-Semitic explanation provided by the Church was strictly limited.

So, the anti-Judaism that had been established and carefully nurtured by the Church became secularized. It was rationalized in the Europe of Enlightenment. It was first developed above all in England and France, where, however, the anti-Semitic, racist elaborations met with relatively little response. Not so in theory-loving Germany. The supposedly rational theory of racist anti-Semitism was still the same old nonsense: anti-Judaistic prejudices covered over with a thin veneer of

168

pseudo-scientific concepts. Yet this was sufficient for many German would-be intellectuals to rationalize their inferiority to Jewish competitors.

Germany's Jews reacted in the usual way to the resurgence of their foes. Only a tiny minority joined the newly emerging Zionist political movement led by Theodor Herzl. Herzl, a Viennese journalist, had realized in the late 19th century that anti-Semites would never be dissuaded from their mania, no matter how patriotic or how humble the Jews became. He was a product of his times, and therefore opted for a solution based on the idea of a nation-state—"the Jewish state."

A larger percentage of the German Jews, however, favored a socio-political solution. These circles, especially enlightened Jewish intellectuals, usually without means, believed that socialism would do away with all social constraints and thus remove the basis on which anti-Semitism could grow. Neither belief was borne out. While Jewish intellectuals were imbibing these self-construed, easy-to-swallow theories, the anti-Semites were increasingly gaining ground.

The bulk of German Jews dealt with anti-Semitism in the conventional manner. The age-old recipe was: *Kein rishes!* (Don't make waves). Whatever you do, do not wake the ostensibly sleeping dragon of anti-Semitism. Unconditional love of the fatherland and the denial of one's own identity ought to do the trick.

A prominent advocate of this way of thinking was the industrialist and journalist Walter Rathenau. In 1905, he wrote a pamphlet entitled "Höre Israel" (Listen, Israel) in which he argued for driving out the anti-Semitic devil with the Beelzebub of self-abasement:

"What has to happen? A race has to consciously educate itself to adapt to outside demands . . . an assimilation in the sense that those inherited characteristics, good or bad, which have shown themselves to be hated by fellow countrymen must be cast off and replaced by more suitable ones."

Rathenau refused to understand that Germany's Jews were

trying with all their might to do what he recommended. But the more they endeavored to ingratiate themselves by assimilating, the more hostile the anti-Semites became. These latter had no desire to have the Jews blend in with them.

To this day, the Jews' strategy of appeasement throughout the world has been based on a cocktail of illogic and wishful thinking. Why have Jews over the centuries always tried to combat anti-Semitic imbecility with "pure reason" and false humility? One answer is that the posture of subservience with a rational touch to it gave Hebrews the impression of retaining a minimum of power in the face of their seemingly all-powerful enemies.

The German Jews—like their fellow Jews in other countries—did not have the strength to recognize the psycho-social dimensions of what was taking shape. In Germany, the danger was especially great, although Jews and others failed to notice it at first. For it was here that anti-Semitism had severed its roots in the Church and was thus more irrational and unruly than elsewhere. Moreover, due to the relatively long period of peace—in other words, a phase without pogroms— German Jews had lost their sensitivity to impending danger.

So, when the threat mounted in the atmosphere of social unrest which followed the defeat in World War I, the response of the Jews was to panic. It was of no help to them that 12,000 Jews had given their lives for Germany, their Fatherland. It made no difference that Walter Rathenau, a German Jew, had done his best to help Germany achieve victory as a head of department in the Prussian Ministry of War. For anti-Semites, he was still the *"Judensau"*—the Jewish swine, and they never stopped calling for his head until a gang of thugs finally turned up to murder him.

Helplessly, the Jews watched their arch-enemy Hitler rise to power.

When Hitler had been in power for half a year, and thousands of German Jews had been maltreated, arrested, thrown out of their jobs or driven into exile, Dr. Löwenstein, chair-

170

man of the Reich Federation of Jewish War Veterans, said: "Fellow soldiers! Germany's honor and *Lebensraum* (living space) are at stake (!). . . True to our steadfast tradition, we shall stand by our Fatherland to the last." In Theresienstadt and other camps, Löwenstein and his fellow soldiers would soon have an opportunity to make good on their promise.

The Nazis were systematic in the way they set about achieving their ends. In 1935, the Nuremberg Laws★ legally degraded Jews to second-class citizens. In 1938, their places of worship were burned down, Jews were maltreated and beaten to death. Yet, hundreds of thousands of German Jews continued to live in their homeland. Many did so because they still believed that the brown-shirted nightmare would pass. Others, like historian Hans Joachim Schoeps, knew "there may be a lot worse to come for German Jews. And the collapse of any illusions as may still exist will have horrible consequences."

Thanks to Hitler and his clan the inner-Jewish debate on strategy—appeasement versus nationalism—was decided by a knockout in favor of the Zionists. The Nazis murdered or drove out German Jewry.

Although 200,000 Jews were vegetating in Germany in 1945, most of them were no longer German Jews, but concentration camp survivors, leftovers from the Nazi death machine, Displaced Persons (DPs). Nearly all of them wanted to leave Germany, the "land of murderers," as quickly as possible. Yet the British and Americans, not to mention all the others, who during World War II had virtually stood by and watched while millions of Jews were being murdered, refused to permit survivors of the genocide to immigrate, not only to their own countries but even to Palestine, whose mandate had been given to London by the League of Nations for the purpose of establishing a "national homeland for Jews" there. Consequently, most Jews in Germany after the Third Reich had no choice but to stay in the country of their oppressors. As soon as the State of Israel was founded in May 1948, however, the majority of the DPs emigrated to the Promised Land.

The Federal Republic of Germany (West Germany) was founded one year later. At first there were about 20,000 Jews living there. Most of them were foreigners, and wanted to emigrate to Israel or to some other country "soon." Hardly any of them fulfilled this wish. Most of them have died in the meantime. Since they did not want to be laid to rest in the land of their families' murderers, they ordered that their bodily remains be buried in the land of their dreams—Israel.

Since Auschwitz, Germany's Jews have been regarded as pariahs by their fellow Jews all over the world. After Israel was founded, the government of the Jewish state and the Zionist World Organization ordered the Jews in Germany to dissolve their community and emigrate en bloc to the Jewish state. With 20,000 Jews still remaining in Germany in 1950, the Israelis tried to force them to come to where they belonged by threatening to take away their identity as Jews if they stayed in Germany.

Worldwide isolation caused the Jews who had stayed in Germany to create a political umbrella organization in 1950, the Central Council of Jews *in* Germany. The very title is a reflection of the consciousness. There had been a time when Jews in Germany tried very hard to be Germans, without too many Germans regarding them as such. After Auschwitz, however, the majority of Jews in this country did not feel at all German any longer. And that is how it has remained to this day!

In 1950, five years after Auschwitz, this attitude was understandable. Today, half a century later, most of the Holocaust survivors have died—as have their murderers. Germany has tried to "make amends" at least for the material damages of the Shoah*. Germany's Jews are enjoying real equal opportunity for the first time in their history. Aside from anti-Semitism, an unusually great measure of benevolence is coming their way. Yet most Jews in this country do not want to be Germans. They even refuse the stubborn desires of "Jew-lovers" to embrace them. Why?

172

It is partly, of course, because of the latent anti-Semitism in the German population—but this anti-Semitism is much the same as it is in comparable countries. However, the main reason lies in the memory of the terrors of the Holocaust. Not only among the survivors, but also among their descendants. What did those who survived have to pass on to their offspring other than a fear of the murderers and their children and their children's children, as well as their own feelings of guilt about living in the midst of these people?

"When I let my hair grow down to my hips, to my parents' dismay, they used to say: Is that what we survived for? When I went out with girls they didn't like—which was just about all of them—they would say: Is that what we survived for? They had only survived for my sake, to bring me into the world. And how did I thank them for it? I tortured them; because of me, they had to ask themselves whether it would not have been better if they had not survived Auschwitz. I felt anger toward my parents and hatred toward myself"—this is Henryk M. Broder's way of describing how the post-Auschwitz generation has been traumatized by the Holocaust through their parents.

The drama of the survivors and their offspring is intensified by a tendency which has become ever more forceful in Jewish life in recent years: to revive the memory of the Holocaust. Instead of honoring the dead and cultivating their memory, the Jews have become side-tracked: the Holocaust itself is becoming the core of a new and false sense of Jewish identity.

Whereas Jewish religion, history, tradition, culture and social life once balanced each other out, concern with the Holocaust has come to dominate Jewish life to an increasing degree in recent years. No wonder. Jews, like the populations among whom they live, are increasingly losing faith in the religion of their fathers. The same is true of their knowledge of history and the tradition of their own community. What remains is the awareness of belonging to the people who were victims.

Books such as Simon Wiesenthal's *Every Day Remembrance*

Day. A Chronicle of Jewish Martyrdom or the credo of Rabbi Marvin Hier, head of the Simon Wiesenthal Center in Los Angeles: "For us here, every night is *Kristallnacht,★*" pave the way for an "intellectual final solution" of Judaism, reducing it to a community that is held together by eternal suffering and grief. If the Holocaust were to take the place of the religious claim to being God's chosen people, Hitler would take God's place as the creator of Jewish being. If the Jews were to become identified with the Holocaust to the exclusion of all else, this would be the ultimate triumph of Adolf Hitler.

In the large Jewish communities of the United States, France, Great Britain or even Israel, there is no reason to fear for the future of Jewish life, despite an increasing fixation on the Holocaust. The cultural, religious and social roots and energies are alive and well there. These vital forces are missing, however, in the community of post-Auschwitz Germany. Pressed between a murderous past, latent anti-Semitism and the attempted embraces of masochistic philo-Semites, Judaism in Germany is in danger of defining itself as a community of victims and of being regarded as such by friend and foe alike.

Are the German friends of the Jews concerned about the well-being of their charges, or are they more concerned about relishing their own feelings of guilt? Don't many of the German philo-Semites resemble butterfly collectors, who have great affection for and a lively interest in the objects of their benevolence, and know a great deal about them, but can deal with them best when they are already preserved—dead, in other words?

I maintain that Germans do not know all that much about living Jews and show little understanding of them and their problems. In postwar Germany, it is certainly easier to buy a book about Jews than to meet a real-live specimen.

Countless books by Jewish authors have been published in Germany since 1945. The works have one conspicuous feature in common: they are all *sterilized of hate*. There is hardly

174

an author living in Germany whose relatives were *not* killed by the Nazis. Yet, there is not a single word of rage against "the Germans" in the books of these authors living in Germany. Is the Jewish *Übermensch* (superhuman) living here, forever kindhearted and forgiving, incapable of sin, much less of revenge, a positive Shylock in a sense, a philo-Semitic creation? One would be tempted to believe this patent nonsense, were it not for books written by Jews outside Germany.

In the works of Primo Levi, Samuel Pisar, Cordelia Edvardson, Ruth Klüger and innumerable others, there is a dynamic process of coming to terms with the murderers and their people. And Germany's Jews? How did they feel when they had to look on as their children and parents, their husbands and wives, their teachers and friends were being slaughtered? Why has no German, not even one of those many experts on Judaism and Jewish literature, ever asked himself in public why Germany's Jews, of all people, never write about their feelings? Can a human being who claims to have a minimum of empathy really imagine that even supposedly aggression-castrated Jews in Germany were never overcome with rage or hatred when they were tortured or when their children were murdered?

Did no one ever wonder why it took more than four decades after Auschwitz for a German Jew to write a Jewish *contemporary* novel (Rafael Seligmann: *Rubinsteins Versteigerung*—Rubinstein's Auction, 1989)? And why the critics in the official Jewish press then got very upset with me for washing our dirty linen in public?

Germany's best-known literary critic, Marcel Reich-Ranicki, himself Jewish, would have us believe that there are no Jewish contemporary novels in Germany because there are no longer any Jewish writers living in either Germany or Austria. Wrong! Reich-Ranicki, the "pope of literary criticism," and his colleagues know very well that a number of talented German-Jewish authors survived Hitler's Reich—Hans Weigel, Hilde Spiel, Friedrich Torberg, for example. Yet none of them has attempted in literary form to come to terms with the life of Jews in Germany after Hitler. The reason is fear.

A credible contemporary novel lives from the feelings and impressions which a writer draws from his environment. But how would the philo-Semites react if they found out that their charges are not bursting with infinite kindness all the time, but are also quite capable of feelings such as rage, anger, hatred and revenge—in short, of "un-Christian" feelings?

The inevitable consequence would be to ask the question feared by Jews in Germany as the devil fears holy water: "Why are you living in Germany?" This question is an explosive device in the consciousness of every Jew who has returned to the land that was once Hitler's Reich. It is a question asked by anti- and philo-Semites, as well as by one's own clan in Tel Aviv or New York, but most searchingly by one's own conscience.

It is not at all impossible, especially for Germans, to understand these Jewish fears. They simply have to make an effort to perceive the problems of Jews in their own country. Only very few are bold enough to do so. Not out of any sense of ill will but out of ignorance, or for fear of unnecessarily hurting the feelings of the tormented souls of the surviving Jews. Apprehensive silence, however, is the worst possible reaction. It leaves the Jews in the ghetto of their fears and the philo-Semites in the wishful realm of their illusions. Provocations can help to shatter the armor of fear: Rainer Werner Fassbinder's* Shylock adaptation, for example, in his play *Garbage, the City and Death*. This finally gave Jews and goyim an opportunity to argue with, against and amongst each other about the role of Jews in Germany.

Instead of being enlivened by argument, the German Jewish relationship is dying of thirst in a sea of indifference, or suffocated by benevolence. For example, Rita Süssmuth (President of the German Parliament), who is a bonafide friend of the Jews, made a point of emphasizing historian

176

Michael Wolffsohn's "patience" with "*us* (!) Germans." This is the same Michael Wolffsohn who proclaims his "German-Jewish patriotism" at every opportunity, even in the titles of books. The ceaseless endeavor to make Jews feel at home in German society cannot be accomplishing very much if the president of the German parliament herself does not consider Wolffsohn, the *Jew*, as one of *us Germans*. Much the same thing has certainly already happened to every Jew in Germany—myself included. *Der Spiegel*,★ for example, published an essay I had written, entitled "The Jews are alive!", in which I focused on the German identity of Jews living here. The response to this in the first published letter to the editor was: "This essay is a wonderful gift from a Jew to us Germans." In other words—You're a nice guy, you gave us Germans a wonderful gift, but since you're a Jew, you're not one of *us*—sorry. Are such remarks merely isolated examples of thoughtlessness, not at all representative of the German effort to integrate Jewish "*Mit*bürger," as they so often say—"*co*-citizens" rather than citizens in their own right? No! These voices are an expression of the general attitude of the Germans *and* of their politicians.

The most impressive and devastating evidence of the way in which Jews are excluded in Germany came in the wake of German reunification. The Soviet Union was falling apart, and as a consequence—a *natural* consequence, one is tempted to say with cynicism—anti-Semitism there was experiencing a revival in all its glory. Hundreds of thousands of Jews fled to Israel. Around 100,000 Russian Jews weighed the possibility of emigrating to Germany. But they did not know the Germans and their politicians very well. Alarmed by the prospect of a Jewish "invasion," the 16 ministers of internal affairs for the German states quickly assembled under the leadership of Wolfgang Schäuble, who was then federal minister of the interior, and imposed, with typically German precision, a limit on the "massive" influx of Jewish immigrants that was looming on the horizon: 10,000 Jewish immigrants per year would be "the tolerance threshold," they said. But it was the ministers who exceeded the "tolerance threshold," not the Jews who wanted to immigrate. These German politicians exposed the hypocrisy in their talk about "German-Jewish reconciliation" and the Jewish "*Mitbürger*"—stressing the "*Mit*" as they always do when the lie becomes apparent, as it does when they refer to non-Germans resident in Germany as "foreign *Mitbürger.*"

As it turned out, setting a limit on the number of ex-Soviet immigrants was unnecessary. Because of the dramatic increase in xenophobic incidents in Germany in the early 1990s, many Russian Jews took fright and decided that Germany was not the place they wanted to go. Applications to move there dropped sharply.

At one time, more than half a million Jews lived in Germany. The "Germanness" of women and men such as Liese Meitner, Albert Einstein, Paul Ehrlich, Max Liebermann, Therese Giehse and other prominent figures is emphasized in Germany today—mainly because they are already dead. But living Jews? Don't we have enough trouble with the 40,000 Hebrews who are already living here? Do we have to bring even more Jews into the country?

As an historical aside, it should be noted that at the same time as they were denying access to Russian Jews, German politicians had no problem with welcoming back home to Germany hundreds of thousands of so-called ethnic Germans living in other countries.

But let us leave aside for a moment the Judeo-centric view!

In Germany, the "intellectual and moral change of attitude" called for by Helmut Kohl when he took office in the early 1980s indeed took place.

Willy Brandt once fell on his knees in Warsaw before a monument to the victims of the Holocaust. A decade later, Kohl, who has a degree in history, strong-armed U.S. President Reagan to go with him to visit the military cemetery in Bitburg,★ where SS officers are also buried. No, Kohl did not want to pay tribute to the gang of murderers that was the SS. But he did want to bring their families back into the fold of the German people—as opposed to living Russian Jews, who would have revitalized the Jewish community in Germany, which is threatened with extinction. But of course the problem with these Jews is that—unlike the dead SS people—they are not Germans!

Since the 1980s, a lot has been happening in Germany. History is being turned upside down like nobody's business. Historian Ernst Nolte★ discovered that Hitler's murder of the Jews was nothing more than the angst-ridden Führer's "fear-driven reaction" to the crimes of the Bolsheviks and the threat they posed to Germany. Nolte does not want to legitimate the killing of the Jews, he says. But he does accuse the Jews of "declaring war on Germany," which at least justified having them detained. In other words, concentration camp, yes, Auschwitz, no? Anyone who thinks Nolte has met with a general wave of outrage, or at least nationwide incomprehension, will be disappointed. There are many people in the world of research, teaching, journalism and politics who share Nolte's opinion.

Reputable German intellectuals are looking for a new role for their new, stronger, united-we-stand fatherland. A great many issues are being debated, such as whether to stay in the various Western and European alliances, or become truly independent. Germans have already shown the world twice what's what. Why not a third time around? After all, the strong one is strongest when he stands alone! And if the world is full of enemies? So what?

Interestingly enough, no one says where the road will lead. Maybe the first step will be to reclaim Königsberg, former capital of East Prussia in what is now Russia?

Exaggerations? Paranoia? If someone had written five years ago that foreigners in Germany would be harassed, humiliated, maltreated and murdered, everyone would have laughed at him—including this writer.

Yet harassment of foreigners and xenophobia did not just appear out of the blue. For a long time, the mainstream "Christian" parties had been warning the populace about the threat from "bogus asylum-seekers," "foreign criminals" and "refugees from poverty" (as if the Germans who emigrated to the U.S. were not refugees from poverty themselves). On top of it, there was all this wretched talk about rejecting a "multicultural society." Had these "Christian Democrats" forgotten that neither Christianity nor democracy nor so many other aspects of our German culture were German inventions? Or that Germany, aside from the 12 years of Nazi rule, has always been multicultural?

When, after half a century, people and synagogues were burning in Germany again, the German people were seized with general dismay. Nobody wanted that to happen! Millions of people lit candles and pilgrimaged to see the Holocaust melodrama *Schindler's List*. One can only hope that they have finally seen the light! So they will see that Jews are not condemned to be sacrificial lambs, that Jews were a vital part of German society, economic life, culture, science and politics for over a milennium. Or at least that Germany's relationship to its Jews and other minorities is a mirror image of the society itself. For the way one treats Jews, women, children and the handicapped is the way in which the members of a society treat each other in general.

And the Jews? The post-Auschwitz generation in any case has decided in favor of living in Germany—even if it is only out of a feeling of inertia. German is our language and our culture, we have German friends and spouses, we work and live *here*—we only go to Israel for vacation. We are Germans, whether we—or anyone else, for that matter—like it or not. And, we have an important function in German society—to sound the alarm whenever there is a need to make people aware of dangers at hand—which is the case at the moment.

One can lament the fact that German Judaism has been reduced to squawking. But that's about as far as it goes, as long as the Germans let hardly any Jews into the country.

On the other hand, it must be said: The present Federal Republic is the most democratic, free, humane and socially just state in German history. It is worth preserving and defending. All people of good will are called upon to do so—Jews and Christians alike.

Is Auschwitz the Yardstick
for Anti-Semitism?

by Henryk M. Broder

In the good old days, everything had its natural order. There were Jews, there were anti-Semites, and the organic connection between the two was anti-Semitism. This aberration was attributed in one case to the proponent's level of education and in another to the time of year. August Bebel considered anti-Semitism to be "the socialism of the dumb guys;" the mayor of Baden, a spa near Vienna with a large Jewish clientele, when asked whether there was any anti-Semitism in his town, liked to answer: "But never during the peak season!"

Things have become much more complicated in the meantime. The natural triangle of Jews, anti-Semitism and anti-Semites has ceased to exist. In countries like Germany and Poland, where large Jewish communities once lived, there are hardly any Jews left. Before World War II, there were more than 3,000,000 of them living in Poland—today there are just 3,000. In Germany prior to 1933, there were over 600,000—today, there are only about 60,000, and this includes the immigrants from the former Soviet Union. In other words, Jews no longer stand out as a relevant part of the population. The same thing goes for the anti-Semites. Around the turn of the century, there were openly anti-Semitic associations, politicians and parties in the German Reich; there was nothing dishonorable about being an anti-Semite. A person was an anti-Semite in the same way as he might be in favor of public floggings, or opposed to the public menace of the Social Democrats' antics, or concerned about the Kaiser's health.

This type of natural anti-Semite no longer exists. When the Jews were wiped out, the self-avowed anti-Semites disappeared as well. Yet anti-Semitism is still around, more or less as a free-floating phenomenon which has lost its subject—and its object.

This is a strange, almost uncanny situation, as if there were no alcohol and no alcoholics, but only alcoholism. And just as the latter is measured in per capita figures on the consumption of spirits, anti-Semitism too, without Jews or anti-Semites, is monitored regularly. The most recent poll by the German Emnid Institute at the beginning of 1994 showed that rather than decline, negative feelings towards Jews have increased in recent years. Thirty-nine percent of those surveyed, for example, were of the opinion that the Jews exploit the Holocaust for their own ends.

And what, a person could ask in all innocence, is actually so anti-Semitic about that opinion? It may simply be wrong, or dumb or silly, but does it necessarily have to be anti-Semitic? It all depends on the definition. The assertion that Jews exploit all sorts of catastrophes for their own ends is part of the repertoire of classical anti-Semitic stereotypes. Be it wars or inflation, the Jews' well-known business acumen makes the most of every situation. And so we have the face of the Jewish profiteer—or rather, the grimacing mug—looming behind the Holocaust. This image is fueled by the desire for exoneration. If, when all is said and done, the Jews can even make a profit from the murder in which they were the victims, then there is really no need to have all that much sympathy with them. The popular claim that everything that happens to the Jews is simply a result of their own behavior belongs in the same category. A former spokesperson of the Green Party, the Berlin attorney Hans-Christian Stroebele, for example, declared in the middle of the Gulf War that the Iraqi missile attacks on Israel were the "logical, almost compelling consequence of Israeli policies." Hardly had Stroebele updated the old anti-Semitic stereotype of the Jews bringing their own misfortune upon themselves than he resigned in order to prevent further damage to his party. He did so protesting vociferously that anti-Semitic thought was totally foreign to him, but he nevertheless stuck to his conviction that if the Israelis had Scud missiles falling into their backyards, it was only because of the way they had treated the Arabs.

There is a vast gray area in which prejudice, lack of knowledge, the wish for historical exoneration, overconfidence and ignorance all add up to a frightfully fertile breeding ground. Not that every careless remark about the Jews automatically qualifies as anti-Semitic, but it does create a climate in which anti-Semitic seeds can take root. The Warsaw correspondent of the German weekly, *DIE ZEIT*, Helga Hirsch, came across a report in the Jewish Historical Institute in Warsaw written by a Jewish *capo* who had turned other Jews over to the German occupying forces during the war. This report, so Helga Hirsch claimed in *DIE ZEIT*, was "uncomfortable for the Jews, who always feel like blameless victims." This can only mean that the Jews are not as blameless as they always make themselves out to be; instead, as victims who bear some of the blame, they also bear some of the responsibility for their fate. Maybe Helga Hirsch did not mean it this way, but language, after all, is there for us to turn thoughts into words, which is why words tell us something about the way we think. This is true not only of Journalists, but also of professors, especially those who teach courses on rhetoric. In a speech given at an awards ceremony for the film *Balagan*, in which an Israeli theater troupe is filmed at work, Professor Walter Jens made the following comment, among others: "To us, the film is one of the most superb treatments of the Holocaust, which is questioned by members of the second generation when it is used only as cement to buttress Israel, and brittle cement at that, since the ideology, the belief in the Holocaust has not been followed up by actions in the direction of making up with the Palestinians." At first, or even second, glance, this is not an anti-Semitic remark, but only rhetorical stew from the "sloppy Joe" department. But if you take a closer look at the individual ingredients, you get a whiff of smoldering resentment behind the ponderous formulation. In Israel, unlike Germany, the Holocaust is not questioned; nor is it a matter of believing in the Holocaust, since it is a fact and not an "opinion." So, in the end, we must deduce from Walter Jens' words that the Holocaust would have only had a meaning if it had prompted the Israelis to make up with the Palestinians. Which is clearly not the case.

If a German journalist places the Jews in the ranks of the victims who are partly to blame for what happened to them, and if a German professor calls upon the Israelis to finally draw the right conclusions from the Holocaust, their statements are first and foremost a good indication of the confusion which reigns even in educated brains when the conversation turns to Jews. How, then, can one hold it against simpler minds if they spread their thoughts among their fellows in unfiltered form, unencumbered by rhetorical formulas? In a lecture, the Dominican father Heinrich Basilius Streithofen described the Jews and the Poles "as the greatest exploiters of the German people." The public prosecutor refused to initiate legal proceedings against Streithofen for defamation and rabble-rousing, claiming that the Father's statements had not been directed against "a part of the domestic population." So where does anti-Semitism start? With a satirical piece in the lampooning German magazine *Titanic*, which printed a fictitious McDonald's ad offering a "Happy Jew Menu" and a "Yellow Star Cheeseburger?" Or with a scholarly article by the historian Ernst Nolte* which speaks of the "intrinsic affinity between Judaism and Bolshevism" and also states that there "can be no denying" the "striking similarity between Zionism and National Socialism?" Is the fictitious ad merely tasteless and the scholarly essay anti-Semitic sophistry in academic disguise?

Sartre called anti-Semitism a "passion." It could also be defined as an addiction. And when it comes to anti-Semitism,

185

just like any other addiction, what counts is the dosage. For one person, a joke may do the trick, whereas another may need to set fire to a synagogue to get his high. It is the same with misogyny and xenophobia. The possibilities range from verbal aggression to grievous bodily harm and murder. In Germany, however, other standards have been established for this. Anti-Semitism is not regarded as a continuum, a transitionless scale of nasty resentments; according to prevailing opinion, anti-Semitism starts with the desecration of cemeteries, with witchhunts against Jews and synagogues being torched. The Munich historian Michael Wolffsohn attaches great importance to the distinction between "real" and "alleged" anti-Semitism, understanding the latter to be verbal blunders, like the statement by one film critic who said that when the Nazis cleared the Cracow ghetto, they were not nearly as cruel as Spielberg made them out to be in *Schindler's List*. And whereas sociologists estimate the anti-Semitic potential in Germany at anywhere from a quarter to a third of the population, the officials in charge of monitoring the phenomenon come up with very different figures. In a speech given at the end of May 1994, Federal Minister of the Interior Manfred Kanther spoke of 8,000 "activists who are openly anti-Semitic." Eight thousand anti-Semites out of a population of 80 million, that's exactly .01 percent of the population. We could happily ignore such a mini-minority and return to business as usual—were it not for the fact that Minister Kanther was talking about only one very specific group, namely the fanatics who desecrate Jewish cemeteries and bemoan the power of World Jewry. He had only one end, the most brutal end, of the anti-Semitic scale in mind. A competent advisor would first have to enlighten him about the fact that there are also well-educated and well-bred armchair anti-Semites who do not wish to be mentioned in the same breath as the desecrators of cemeteries. So where does anti-Semitism start? How does one recognize an anti-Semite who does not happen to be scrawling "Death to the Jews!" on a wall, or de-molishing a grave?

Meanwhile, as was only to be expected, the courts are try-ing to find an answer to this question. A journalist felt that he had been libeled by being called a "left-wing anti-Semite" and sued. He won the case in a lower Hamburg court. Thus, for what was probably the first time in German legal history, a court decided that accusing someone of being anti-Semitic—in this case, in its left-wing variant—amounted to libel or slander and was not covered by the right to freedom of ex-pression in public debate. The court case is noteworthy for several reasons. First of all, in the course of the hearings the court established a sort of "statute of limitations" applicable to books. The book that had caused its author to be called a "left-wing anti-Semite" had been published many years be-fore, and you "can't rub an author's nose in a book he wrote 20 years ago." Secondly, when delivering its written state-ment, the court endeavored to establish binding and generally valid standards for a person to qualify as an "anti-Semite" and/or as a "left-wing anti-Semite." The court conceded that left-wing anti-Semitism was not the same as Nazi anti-Semi-tism, but then it turned around and blurred this distinction by establishing that "the person so designated was categorized as an anti-Semite per se;" for "Auschwitz is inconceivable with-out anti-Semitism" and classifying the plaintiff [the journalist] as someone who "thinks in a manner . . . which made such a thing possible" meant, "in absolute terms," that "the person in question pays tribute to a *weltanschauung* which made geno-cide possible." In absolute terms, this ruling means that Auschwitz and anti-Semitism are equated with each other, and that Auschwitz is the standard for measuring anti-Semi-tism. By setting the standard so high, however, all other vari-ants of anti-Semitism have no problem getting through. For example, anyone who does not want to gas the Jews but merely wants to exclude them from social life can forthwith cite the Hamburg ruling and take legal action against being categorized under a particular view of the world which had genocide as its objective. This ruling could be regarded as a case where something went wrong because the issue was simply over the heads of the judges in question—were it not indicative of a trend which can hardly be explained away by pointing to the deficiencies of individual judges. In a case brought against a high functionary of the neo-fascist NPD (National Party of Germany) who believes that the systematic destruction of the Jews in the Third Reich is a lie that is spread as propaganda, a court in the city of Mannheim not only declared that the accused was a "responsible person with a clear set of principles" whose political convictions "came straight from the heart" but also cleared him of suspicion for something which seemed so obvious: he was "on the political right," found the court, but he was "not an anti-Semite in the sense of Nazi racist ideology." If a practicing right-wing extremist who denies that there was a Holocaust is not an anti-Semite, then who is? Presumably only someone who himself killed Jews or would welcome the chance.

Thus, the unique and unprecedented nature of Auschwitz is being used in the meantime to make milder forms of anti-Semitic madness socially acceptable and tolerable. But if Auschwitz is the litmus test for anti-Semitism, then all other standards cease to exist. In the eyes of the minister of the interior, anti-Semites are a sort of informal association with 8,000 members; in the eyes of a court, only potential perpetrators of genocide are anti-Semites, and no decent person would want to have anything to do with them. There's nothing in-between. In this manner, anti-Semitism is disposed of, removed from the midst of society and deposited on the fringes, as if on a waste dump that nobody wants to have near their own front door.

Free-floating anti-Semitism without Jews on the one hand and without avowed anti-Semites on the other defies all attempts to pretend that it is not there. Can there not be a third alternative, somewhere between the impossibility of solving a

188

problem and the wish to ignore it? In the United States, the tendency is to find a way to live with intractable problems. Nobody there denies that anti-Semites and anti-Semitism exist. And the Jews there take in stride the role of the scapegoat that is assigned to them. Anti-Semitism, they say, well, anti-Semitism is when people can stand us even less than is actually natural.

The Repeating of the Cycle
Russian Jews in Germany

by Peter Ambros

Sasha is not really a typical name for a barber in Berlin. And indeed, Sasha, who has been cutting my hair for the past 20 years, belongs to a minority among Berliners—although in the meantime this group forms a majority of the Jewish community in Berlin—who are referred to simply, but rather vaguely, as "Russian Jews." Sasha himself chats to me in German while he is parting my hair on the left, then in Russian to the next customer, who is having his hair washed by Sasha's stout blond-haired wife, and then again in Lithuanian to her. But 20 years ago—as he once told me with a grin—his elder son, who was born back in Kovno, had been the first child in many, many years to baffle the other four year-olds on the playground of Berlin's Jewish day-care center, and the teachers as well, by speaking perfect Yiddish.

For the newcomers to the Jewish community in Germany who have come from the countries of the former Soviet Union—some 15,000 over the past five years—the label "Russian Jews" is just as imprecise (and in Germany, people are sticklers for precision) as "German Jews" is for the "old established" Jews who settled between the Elbe and Rhine rivers and on the Havel only 30 years earlier than the so-called "new immigrants" of today. The "real" German Jews who are still around can be found today in Rechavia in Jerusalem, in Queens, New York, and especially in Fort Lauderdale, Florida. This does not mean that their grandparents and great grandparents did not come from Kovno, Odessa or Kasrelivke. For, as far as the Jewish population is concerned, Germany was already a country of immigrants 100 years before the Declaration of Independence of the United States of America was signed.

Were there ever really any Russian Jews who deserved this name by German standards of precision? This question will not seem quite as absurd as it does at first glance after we have made a short excursion into history, and it might even be expanded to include German Jews—as we have already implied and will soon find out. The historical retrospective will first take us back to a time more than 1,000 years ago, to the legendary land of the Khazars between the Caspian Sea and the Black Sea. Threatened by the influx of Christian Orthodox missionaries to the north and by Islamic missionaries to the south—which is to say, under threat of external domination—the shrewd ruler of the Khazars, King Bulan, came up with the idea, immortalized in poetry by Yehuda Halevi, of having his people circumcised and tauntingly proclaiming: Haha, since we are Jews we already believe in one God, so we are unsuitable material for missionary work!

The idea was such a big hit in the region that the patriarchs of then neighboring Russia soon feared that it would undermine the ideological basis of the Kiev state. Their response was to establish a state doctrine of unsurpassed rigidity, to which Russia remained loyal up until modern times. It proclaimed that Jews were much too dangerous for Russia to tolerate their presence on its sovereign territory. In practice, this meant that, with every new conquest in the growing Czarist empire, Jews living in the newly conquered territory were first of all confronted with the choice: conversion to Christianity or death. The third option was to flee.

Ironically, it was this exclusively *judenrein* empire, 'cleansed of all Jews,' which, when Poland was carved up some 200 years ago, took over control of the region with the world's highest concentration of Jews—the area stretching from the Carpathian mountains of the eastern Tatra in the north all the

191

way to Transylvania in the south, later the home of Tevye the milkman. Why did Russia at that time not resort to the solution which was later to be masterminded by Adolf Hitler, namely to use mass murder as a means to make this vast area free of Jews? Was it because the Czar had qualms, or because Russia lacked the technological know-how for this task? We shall never know. The Russian compromise solution was called the Pale of Settlement—an early-modern form of apartheid in which the new territory as a whole was more or less hermetically cordoned off, like a huge Jewish "homeland" in Eastern Europe. The result of this policy was that during the 19th century, at the height of Jewish assimilation in Europe, the so-called "Russian Jews" were the only "Jewish Jews" left because no one was there to whom they could have assimilated.

The parallel history of the German Jews happened in reverse, so to speak. On the eve of the Modern Age, the German states—a collection of large, small and very small countries—were also virtually free of Jews. During the Middle Ages, they first managed to sap their Jews dry financially and then drove them out (following the example already set, incidentally, by the English, the French and, of most recent fame, the Spanish). However, Germany emerged from the Thirty Years' War a depopulated country, and nowhere more so than Prussia, whose Pyrrhic victory had created a desperate shortage of subjects in general, and economically active subjects in particular. The Prussian rulers therefore brought into the country minorities who were oppressed in other places: French Huguenots, Protestants from Salzburg and Bohemia, and also Jews. This marked the beginning of a tragic road which ended in Auschwitz, and in retrospect, the word "symbiosis" as a description of the process has a cynical ring to it. In the 1980s, the late Heinz Galinski, then chairman of the Central Council of Jews in Germany (note the small but important difference: not "of German Jews"—nothing beats precision!), referred to it as a dramatic encounter—Jewishness and Prussianness, a cultural tradition without a state and a state without a cultural tradition.

Perhaps it was precisely because the unifying cultural symbols of the state were so newly hatched and relatively thin on substance, that such painstaking attention was devoted in the Prussian "melting pot" to absolute compliance with the "Prussian way of life," enforced, if need be, by sneaking glances through the neighbors' drawn curtains. The German proclivity for precision was an added factor, and thus emerged a 200-year cycle which was given a name, with truly German precision, by the organizers of the "Jewish Worlds" super-exhibition presented in Berlin in 1992. As they put it in the catalogue, Germany demanded of its Jewish immigrants a "soundless adaptation."

In practical terms, the cycle functioned more or less like this: A young man breaks out of a shtetl, a ghetto in the Pale of Settlement. He is a lot like the character of the Fixer in the film version of Malamud's story by the same name, which was based on the experiences of a real person whose name was Mendl Beilis. In contrast to Malamud's Fixer and the real Beilis, who only barely escaped execution for a ritual murder in Kiev after a long period of incarceration and torture, our young man does not go east but instead crosses the Russian border into Prussia. After peddling for a while as an Eastern Jew in Germany, he sets up shop in a permanent booth in Berlin's *Scheunenviertel* or shanty town; and when he dies and is given a traditional Jewish burial, he leaves to his son a shop that is doing good business. The son, for his part, reaches the height of his career as a factory owner, speaks German without an accent, though he enjoys throwing in a few words of Yiddish when he talks about how business has gone that week over the shabbos meal. And his son, in turn, could resemble Albert Ballin (not to be confused with Beilis!), that super-rich shipowner in Bremen, who was such a close friend of the Hohenzollern Kaiser Wilhelm II that he took his own life on November 9, 1918, out of grief over Wilhelm II's abdication and the fall of the German Empire. It goes without saying that Ballin himself would have classified the Beilis-types who migrated to Germany during Ballin's lifetime—and who were therefore carbon copies of his own grandfather—as "disturbingly exotic Eastern Jews." Moreover, this third, soundlessly adapted generation could usually afford to dedicate their children to intellectual rather than financial pursuits, which is what made possible the symbiosis of German and Jewish intellect, to which reference was so often made right up until the Holocaust.

In Germany as well as in Russia, Jewish history achieved a catharsis in our century of progress. Just like the bourgeois emancipation of the Jews about 100 years earlier—only a bit more intensely, perhaps, and without fear of resorting to overt violence—Bolshevism offered the Jews equality and discreetly hid in the fine print of the footnote to the new social contract that the price of the *égalité* they had gained would be to give up their own identity. Three generations of socialist contentment in the Soviet Union were sufficient to transform what used to be the last "Jewish Jews" of Europe into "Russian Russians," not soundlessly by any means and virtually bypassing a "Russian Jews" stage. What was still Jewish about most of the Tevyes' and Beilises' progeny was the entry in their passports—not to be found anywhere else but Israel: Nationality—Jewish.

At the same time, Hitler's Germany was busily tending to the business of physically eliminating its "citizens of Mosaic belief," who had already had to shed their identity in the process of soundless adaptation during the previous century. After May 8, 1945, when the nightmare was over, there were survivors—usually Polish Jews—who resurrected the Shabbos service in the ruins of Berlin, Munich and Frankfurt. Those who condemned them, or the emigrants who later returned to East Germany from Great Britain and the United States, for their willingness to make their home at the epicenter of

194

the catastrophe that had just been overcome, should stop and consider. Consider the fact, for example, that they survived the concentration camps even though the countries of the West would not take them in during their hour of need. Or the fact that they were able to survive although the Allies did not waste a single bomb on the death camps or the railway lines leading to them, even after they already knew what was going on there. The fact that the Jewish communists who returned to East Germany believed that, in the German workers' and peasants' state, they would find a refuge from McCarthyism. And anyone who thinks that the place for Jews to go since 1948, if not before, is the Jewish state, Eretz Yisrael, must know that, after Israel declared its independence, David ben Gurion waited just as much in vain for Jews to come from France and the United States as he did for those from Germany. A Zionist, as we know, is a Jew who gives another Jew money so that a third Jew can emigrate to Palestine.

The Israeli military victory of 1967 was a turning point in the consciousness of all Jews in the world, not least of all as an answer to the sometimes mute, sometimes openly expressed self-reproach that "allowing oneself to be led like lambs to the slaughter" was a trait of the Jewish national character. In most of the Western countries, the new awareness led to a situation in which practicing Judaism was replaced by admiration for the Jewish state as a surrogate identity. In concrete terms, this often meant that one's own Jewish identity was reduced to the practice of Zionism as defined above.

This was not the case in the Soviet Union. Here, where the practice of Judaism had already come to an end two generations before as a consequence of pressure from the state, the Jewish victory over Arab armies backed by Soviet military advisers led to a euphoria of self-affirmation, the first white spot on the black smear in the passport, the stigmatizing word "Jew." In 1968–69, when the first Zionist swallows began to arrive from the Soviet Russian empire, no one in Israel was willing to believe their stories of how widespread the desire to emigrate from Russia might become. Israelis had long since resigned themselves to the process of Sovietization of the Jews in the land of the Bolsheviks. The call to "Let my people go!", which rang out from the western Jewish world to Moscow, only gradually took hold, and in retrospect, in all fairness to the truth, it must be said that those who were issuing the call did not expressly add 'where to.'

It is generally known that the goods produced in the socialist Eastern bloc countries were divided into three categories: the top-quality goods which were exported to the West, the low-quality products which went to the other bloc countries and the rejects which were foisted onto the domestic population. This is what is meant by the joke that was going around in the USSR during the 1970s: "Why are Jewish children who are born in the Soviet Union better-looking than non-Jewish children? Because they are made for export." The last 15 years of the Soviet state were accompanied by a wave of Jewish emigration to the Promised Land on such a scale that it, in turn, produced an abundance of Jokes in Israel, the gist of which is perhaps summed up most concisely in the following question and answer: "What will Israel's second official language be in the year 2000? Ivrit [Hebrew], of course."

For Soviet Jews, leaving the Soviet Union meant embarking on a journey into the free world. Is it any wonder, then, that some of them felt free to make their own choice as to where to live in the free world? And at that time, from the vantage point of Moscow, Kiev, Leningrad or Riga, Berlin was the closest city in which the rules of the free world applied—and also the closest to family members left behind. Moreover, Germany was and still is one of the more prosperous European countries with a comprehensive social security system, and—as a result of its coming to terms with the National Socialist past—Germany was also a country with an unusually liberal right to asylum. Anyone who has ever had to make the dramatic decision to emigrate—with or without the

196

responsibility of providing for a family—will understand why such credentials can make a country an attractive destination for emigration. This attraction was also discovered 20 years ago by our acquaintance and my barber Sasha.

What all this comes down to is that, up until five years ago, the great- and great great-nephews of Mendl Beilis who wished to emigrate from the Soviet Union had two alternatives to choose from: either to accept the invitation to a country which promised them a proud and free but in all likelihood difficult life, or to travel uninvited to one of the other countries which, although promising nothing, offered the prospect of prosperity and riches to those who worked hard. As far as Germany was concerned, this situation unexpectedly changed in an important respect at the same time as the socialist Eastern bloc in Europe collapsed.

On March 18, 1990, the still existing German Democratic Republic (East Germany), in its only free election, elected the first and last democratic parliament in its history, called the 'Volkskammer' (People's Chamber). At that time, the slowly disintegrating state had another six months of formal existence left before German unification. And one of the first actions taken by the freely elected Volkskammer was something which no West German parliament has ever done to the present day, namely to apologize to the Jewish people for the crimes of the Nazi period and to invite all Jews who feel threatened wherever they may be living to come to the German Democratic Republic. (It was Elie Wiesel, incidentally, who accused West Germany shortly before, in November 1988, in a speech in West Berlin, of having failed to make this most self-evident and natural of gestures; the same Elie Wiesel who, three years earlier, had asked President Reagan, in vain, not to visit the SS cemetery in Bitburg.★)

So, alongside Israel, Germany thus became the second country to extend an invitation to Beilis' great-grandchildren. At the same time, the Soviet Union was to survive under this name for only a little more than a year, and the traditional

197

breed of anti-Semitism became increasingly overt in the economically and politically disintegrating country, and also increasingly clear in the areas of art, culture and science. For this reason, thousands of Jews in the Soviet Union accepted the East German invitation; and on October 3 of that same year—on the Day of German Unity—the Federal Republic of Germany acquired, as Czarist Russia once did when Poland was partitioned, the area with the highest concentration of Jews in Germany at that time, namely East Berlin.

Let us come back to Sasha. Twenty years ago I ran into him in a large men's hairdressing salon in Charlottenburg—the center of what was then West Berlin. He was working there for a wage, since his master hairdresser's certificate from the Soviet Union was not recognized in Berlin. I became a steady customer of his and had a chance to learn something new about the Russian colony every time I had my hair cut. I was away from the city for two years in the early 1980s, and when I came back, Sasha was not working in the salon any more. After awhile, I came across a tiny barber's shop called "Sasha's" a few blocks away from where he had worked before. My barber had in practice become self-employed; he was preparing to take the German master hairdressers' exam and was running the store de jure as the branch of a business owned by a Berlin master hairdresser, to whom he paid an annual fee based on the latter's tax return. When the Berlin Chamber of Trades failed Sasha for the third time, I began to suspect that something was amiss and asked him to tell me more about the payment arrangements. Sasha showed me the documents, and I could hardly believe my eyes when I found out that the boss of the phony company was having my Jewish hairdresser pay tax to the Protestant church. I tried to persuade him to ask the Jewish Community, where he was and still is a member, to intervene on his behalf. Sasha refused to do so, and one year later he finally got his master hairdresser's certificate. Incidentally, before the last elections to the representative assembly of the Jewish Community, I asked him why the Russians, who for a long time now have made up the numerical majority of the Community's membership, did not put up a larger number of their own candidates for the election. Sasha just laughed. "If we were in charge of things," he replied, "that would mean the end of order in the Community, and things are fine just the way they are." In other words, we have learned to respect the fact that precision is important in Germany. Is this the way our friend Beilis, with the booth in the *Scheunenviertel*, might have acted and replied a hundred years ago? I think so.

In other words, the old cycle is repeating itself, but not quite according to the same old pattern. Most of the immigrants in recent years, since the invitation from East Berlin and the outbreak of undisguised anti-Semitism in the Russian culture industry, come from different professional strata than most of the newcomers in the preceding 20 years. Judaism in Germany, as we have seen, traditionally did not produce intellectuals until the fourth generation. But the Jewish community has not been around for that many generations in today's Germany. Their intellectual background and the fact that their parents did not allow themselves be "led like lambs to the slaughter"— indeed some of them were officers in the Soviet army who freed the survivors of the concentration camps in 1945—are responsible for the main difference in mentality between the new immigrants and the "old-established" immigrants who have lived here for years—which, from the vantage point of the former, also includes Sasha and his family.

Shortly after the end of the war, U.S. General Lucius D. Clay once stated in Berlin that, one day, democracy in Germany would be measured in terms of the degree to which Jewish life is possible there. From today's perspective, this statement could be turned around and expanded. Tomorrow it might be possible to say that German democracy can be measured in terms of how far the traditional cycle of Eastern Jews will be possible in German Jewish life without the need for soundless adaptation.

Mixed Marriages in Germany—
Cause for Concern?

by Elvira Grözinger

On May 30, 1994 the German daily *Frankfurter Allgemeine Zeitung* reported the following news item under the headline "Clinton's brother-in-law weds in the White House Rose Garden:" ". . . The President and First Lady arranged the wedding ceremony for Tony Rodham, Hillary Clinton's brother, and Nicole Boxer, daughter of Senator Barbara Boxer. After invocations by a Methodist minister and a representative of the Jewish community, the 26-year-old bride and the President's 39-year-old brother-in-law (. . .) took their vows."

This casual announcement would seem to indicate that "mixed" marriages—between different faiths—are taken in stride in the United States and are probably not uncommon, even in the upper echelons of society. In Germany, on the other hand, which now has a Jewish population of about 42,000, interfaith marriages are officially considered to be the exception. Nevertheless, there is still talk—sometimes in whispers, sometimes quite openly—about very high numbers. In his article on "The Situation of the Jews in Today's Germany," Micha Brumlik quotes the Jewish Press Service of 1985: ". . . the Jewish Community in the Federal Republic is forced to grapple with the highest rate—nearly 65 percent—of mixed marriages among Jewish communities worldwide."

In a discussion with Jewish young people and students, a young officiating rabbi in Germany recently expressed the opinion that "mixed marriages are a Holocaust for the Jewish people." Another Israeli rabbi made a similar observation on a visit to Germany. Although this view does not go uncontradicted, it nonetheless indicates how controversial and topical the issue of mixed marriages has become in the inner-Jewish discussion today.

The Jewish journalist Peter Sichrovsky confronts the touchy subject head on in his article "Memory as a Burden," but I believe he approaches it from a completely wrong angle by interpreting mixed marriages as a reaction to the Holocaust: ". . . Since National Socialism, it is not persecution and expulsion which have become the basis of Jewish identity, but annihilation itself, and that is a fatal and life-negating basis. In recent years, there has been much lamenting over the high percentage of mixed marriages among Jews. Many seem to want to escape from the spiritual ghetto of destruction and annihilation and look for a way out by marrying people of other religions. This may have less to do with the possibilities of finding a Jewish partner than with the life-negating brainwashing by the terror of remembering the Holocaust."

Mixed marriages, however, are by no means a recent phenomenon, much less a product of the Holocaust, a fact which needs to be emphasized. Indeed, mixed marriages are obviously one of the oldest concerns of the Jewish powers-that-be; why else would such alliances be explicitly forbidden in the Bible and considered to be invalid? In Deuteronomy 7:3, it says on the subject of Gentiles: "You shall not make marriages with them, giving your daughters to their sons or taking their daughters for your sons." And Ezra 9:2–3 proves that, even in those days, the Jews did not obey: ". . . 'For they have taken some of their daughters to be wives for themselves and for their sons; so that the holy race has mixed itself with the peoples of the lands. And in this faithlessness the hand of the officials and chief men has been foremost.' When I heard this, I rent my garments and my mantle, and pulled hair from my head and beard, and sat appalled."

The majority of the older-generation Jews living in Germany today originally came from eastern Europe, which may be one reason why they are so frequently and categorically against the plans of their children and grandchildren to marry outside the faith. In many cases, these eastern Europeans were raised in the Orthodox tradition and still observe the Talmud, which is very strict on the matter (in the *Avoda zara* and *Kiddushin* tractates, for example). Thus, according to Jewish law, the Jewish partner in a mixed marriage does not have to get a divorce before marrying again, since the first marriage was not valid in the first place. On the other hand, a divorce is necessary if the non-Jewish partner, or both partners, in the first marriage converted to Judaism before they were married. But even if the Jewish partner converts to a non-Jewish religion thereafter, a divorce is still necessary before he or she can marry again. If one of the partners converted to Judaism after the marriage, this marriage is considered to be a mixed marriage and is not valid; the children from such a marriage are therefore illegitimate.

In my own circle of friends and acquaintances, there have been a lot of mixed marriages, and virtually none of them have ended in divorce as a result of religious differences. In other words, they are permanent relationships which have lasted for many years, between converts and non-converts and partners who are Jewish by birth. Recently, in an empirical study on mixed marriages, I asked some of the people involved to relate their experiences and impressions. Most of them were more than willing to answer my questions at length; a few saw no need to give an opinion on the subject since they regard their marriage as absolutely natural and normal; only one couple, who have been friends of mine for 15 years, flatly refused to fill out my questionnaire. The man (Jewish from eastern Europe) did not want to comment since his wife converted to Judaism before they got married, which is why he simply marked "interconfessional marriage" as "not applicable." His mother, who has passed away in the meantime, never accepted her daughter-in-law, even after she converted. This case shows that, in some marriages of many years, the question of mixed marriages is still a painful one. This is also why the partners who convert (usually the women) often go out of their way to be accepted as Jews, an effort which sometimes seems exaggerated and forced, making the already difficult process of integration into the Jewish community even more difficult for them.

After German reunification, it turned out that even the small number of East German Jews were for the most part living in mixed marriages. In the case of the older generation, it was often a matter of Jews who had emigrated during the war and who later returned to what they believed was the "better" Germany. As avowed Communists, they did not assign much value to Jewish religion and tradition. So, as in the case of all Jews from the former Communist countries, it is meaningless to speak in terms of "interconfessionalism" since religion was not practiced nor even always tolerated by the society in which they lived at the time. As a result, their children were hardly, if at all, exposed to Judaism. Now that Jewish communities and regional councils have been established in the eastern part of Germany and Jewish life, complete with rabbis and synagogues, is gradually taking shape, in a few of these mixed marriages the non-Jewish partner has made the effort to convert. The children of these marriages are now Jewish and can be brought into the fold. Naturally, the Jewish communities are open to them and the Jewish establishment hopes that many of them will opt for Judaism.

The situation is different for children whose mothers have not converted. The Central Welfare Office of Jews in Germany provides social services for the communities, as well as assistance in the integration of immigrants, care for the elderly and youth services. Recreational activities are organized for the children and young people, but only children recognized as Jewish are allowed to take part in them. Children from mixed marriages in which the mother is not Jewish are not allowed to take part in these activities, although in large communities, many of them go to Jewish schools. In some cases, this restrictive policy makes the affected families so angry and frustrated that they turn away from the community altogether. Unfortunately, there is no other Jewish community that can take them in, for the simple fact is that in Germany there is only one, unified and Orthodox community; those isolated groups which try to practice a different kind of Judaism exist on a private level. I personally consider that it is important and makes a lot more sense to cultivate an appreciation of Jewish tradition in these children so that they will eventually decide in favor of Judaism, especially since their parents are already attempting to guide them in this direction. However, it is felt within the communities that it is up to the mothers of these children to convert if they want to spare their children this kind of conflict. In any case, I find it counterproductive to punish the children for something that is beyond their control, especially in view of the fact that a growing number of young Jews are becoming disaffected with Jewish life. Not only is the community missing an opportu-nity to stem this development; it is actually hastening it along.

At this point, I would like to convey some of the impressions related to me by people with personal experience of mixed marriage. For the most part, these marriages are based on mutual tolerance, but lean in favor of Judaism; in other words, the non-Jewish partner tends to be more tolerant than the Jewish partner.

A German-Jewish woman, herself the child of a Jewish mother and non-Jewish father, is now divorced; she raised her now adult son as a single parent. The divorce had nothing to do with religious differences. As a result of the Shoah★, there was not a very large selection of Jewish partners in her generation. Before getting married, the man had said he would convert, but after they were married, he changed his mind. When their child was small, her husband insisted on spending the Christmas holidays with his family. Although he agreed to have his son circumcised, he went on a pleasure trip abroad at the time of the ceremony—something a Jewish father would not have done. After the divorce, the father did not have much to do with his son, and the child was then raised in the Jewish tradition by his mother. The son says he himself would never marry a non-Jewish woman since he would like to have a Jewish household. The mother now sees no alternative to a mono-religious marriage. She feels that mixed-faith marriages lead to conflicts which are carried over to the children, so a decision should be made in favor of one religion or the other.

A non-Jewish German who has been married to a Jewish woman for over a quarter of a century and brought up his now adult daughter in the liberal Jewish tradition says that he has come to see many things differently from the way he saw them before the marriage and he would agree with the opinion expressed by the woman described above. After awhile, it became clear to him that preserving cultural differences between his wife and himself would eventually cause a rift between them. He realizes that cultural-religious stability can only be maintained if one partner completely adapts to the other. So, in his case, he completely adapted to his Jewish wife, which gave him the harder task on the one hand, but enriched him on the other. It took longer for him to become fully accepted by the Jews than for his wife to be accepted by the non-Jews. Neither of the two families had any problem accepting the marriage. He pointed out that cultural differences become more pronounced the older one gets and the longer one is married, which is why the partners should reach an agreement on the question of religion before conflicts arise.

His wife is not particularly religious, but preserves Jewish tradition. She, too, is doutbtful that their marriage would last if they were not so tolerant of each other and willing to meet halfway. She sees a necessity for children to be raised in the Jewish tradition, because of the need to bolster the Jewish population since the Shoah. This is also why the problem of mixed marriages and the weakening of cultural-religious Jewish identity should not be taken lightly. She is happy to share and learn about Judaism with her husband, just as she also enjoys learning about her husband's cultural background against the European background they have in common. The child was also raised in a tolerant environment, but in the Jewish tradition. She says it would be more difficult for her to live with a Christian or Moslem who practiced his religion. The only reason she would like her husband to convert to Judaism is so that they could be buried together ("when we are 120 years old . . .").

A young man born in Germany has a Jewish father and a mother who converted to Orthodox Judaism before getting married. His parents raised him in the Jewish faith and he feels it is important to preserve the Jewish community. He would like to have a Jewish marriage partner. This is what most of the younger Jewish men (about 25 years old) told me, by the way; many of them had non-Jewish girlfriends but did not want to marry them.

One woman born in Germany after the war married a non-Jewish man who has understanding for her involvement in the Jewish community. He is not a practicing Christian. The couple does not have any children, but both feel that if there are children in a marriage, the parents should agree on their religious upbringing; she thinks that children may become neurotic if they grow up in an environment troubled by conflicts over religion. A marriage between two people with the same religion is preferable. Their own marriage is based on mutual tolerance, although the non-Jewish partner tends to give in more. The woman's father, an East European Jew, did not approve of his daughter's marriage and has hardly any contact with her husband's family. Unfortunately, this is not an isolated case, since many parents from eastern Europe do not accept their non-Jewish daughter-in-law, with the consequence that they have little or no contact with their grandchildren, although such contact would certainly help to

206

strengthen the Jewish tradition. This is frequently the reason why the parents of these children are so unhappy about being rejected, since the grandparents could convey to the children the Jewishness which they themselves are unable to impart. Another missed opportunity!

A second woman who was born in Germany after the war has been living with a non-Jewish German for over ten years in a common-law marriage. She is actively involved in the Jewish community; he is a non-practicing Christian. She thinks it is better to look for a partner with the same religion, but if that does not work out, then both partners must be tolerant enough of each other to live together. She and her partner have no children, which eliminates a lot of problems.

As we can see from these responses, tolerance for one another in matters of religion is absolutely essential in order for a partnership of this kind to work, and it helps if one partner adapts to the other. So it is somewhat unusual to find a marriage between a practicing German Christian and a practicing Jewish woman from Israel. This couple has been married for several years. The children (from the woman's first marriage, to a Jew) are being raised in the Jewish faith, and the non-Jewish partner actively supports her. There are occasional conflicts, during the Gulf War, for example, when her husband was closer to the peace movement and she leaned more to the other side. The families of both partners are still distant towards the relationship.

A Jewish woman from eastern Europe, born after the war and living in Germany since 1968, has been married to a non-Jewish German for many years. They have two children who were not raised in the Jewish faith. Neither of them actively practices their religion, but she still has ties to the Jewish tradition. She is in favor of monoreligious marriage and this is what she wishes for her children. In her opinion, it is better for Jews to have a Jewish spouse. The families did not approve of the marriage, although over time, they have become less negative about it.

An emphatic appeal for a free choice of partners comes from a Jewish man from eastern Europe, who also came to Germany in 1968 and has been married to a Catholic woman from his native country for 30 years. They have two children. Religious differences do not play a role in this marriage. The reactions on the part of their families and their environment in eastern Europe ranged from neutral to aggressive; as foreigners in Germany, they have had other problems to deal with. Since the children were not raised in one belief or the other, the couple is neutral on this issue. The husband himself would not want to influence them in any way when it comes to choosing a partner.

Most of the people surveyed emphasized that love and not religion is the decisive factor when choosing a partner. This is exactly what Stanislav Jerzy Lec, the Polish Jewish aphorism writer, meant when he said, "Wie die Hormone, so der Mormone . . ."—the Mormons follow their hormones—it all comes down to "chemistry." A constantly recurring explanation for why Jewish men or women end up with a non-Jewish partner is that the small Jewish community in Germany does not offer enough of a partner selection. This is one of the main reasons why Jewish immigrants from the former Soviet Union are welcome, since they bring "fresh blood" to the communities. But I also know a few Jews with parents from eastern Europe who talked their children out of love-matches with non-Jews by emotionally blackmailing them and threatening to commit suicide if they went through with their plans—and this despite the lack of more suitable partners and even before the Russian immigrants revived the marriage market.

Why do mixed marriages seem to constitute even more of a problem in Germany than in other countries? Perhaps part of the answer lies in recent history: the awareness of what happened between 1933 and 1945 and the realization that non-Jewish parents or grandparents—the in-laws, in other words—may have a share in the guilt.

This "history factor" became especially acute when young Germans discovered the "Atonement Initiative" during the 1960s and the possibility of studying or working in the kibbutzim, often out of protest against their parents. To make their contribution to a new beginning in the history of German-Jewish relations, many of them went to Israel, where they found Jewish partners. Some of these visitors to Israel stayed there, but most of them returned to Germany with their partners. The majority of Israeli or Jewish wives adjusted to life in Germany better than the Israeli men did, and the marriages with German men turned out to be relatively stable, whereas many of the marriages with German women fell apart. In many cases, the Israeli men eventually abandoned their German wives and children and went back to Israel by themselves. However, there are also a number of cases in which German women left their Israeli husbands in Israel and came back to Germany with their children. I suspect that the marriages did not work out because the cultural differences were simply too great, since Sabras are often "Oriental" in behavior, even if they are of European descent. The marriages that took place after the Six Day War were also often based on false, romantic ideas: Israeli soldiers were seen as "heroes," for example, but many turned out to be tyrants and paper-tigers at home; and German women, desired at first as blond trophies by the dark-haired Israelis, eventually lost their special appeal.

To sum up, I would say that each person should do "whatever makes him (or her) happy." There are no pat solutions, and as history has shown us, it does no good to make rules. Even so, a few small Italian Jewish communities can give us food for thought. In Mantua, for example, where famous Jewish printers once lived, Jewish life recovered slightly after World War II. In the meantime, however, it has all but disappeared because the postwar generation has married outside the faith, the Catholic partners have drawn the children away from Judaism and raised them as Catholics. Since there are more Catholics than Jews in the world, this should serve as both a warning and an incentive to foster and preserve Jewish identity in the younger generation.

The Development of Jewish Religious Life in Postwar Germany

by Micha Brumlik

1.

Prior to 1933, the religious life of the almost 500,000 Jews in Germany was characterized by great diversity. On the one hand, there were large *Einheitsgemeinden* (united communities) which followed predominantly liberal or reformist practices; on the other, there was the separatist Orthodoxy which had attempted, ever since the end of the 19th century, to bring traditional Orthodox life in line with bourgeois culture and German national consciousness on the basis of the teachings of Samson Rafael Hirsch. There were thus two forms of Orthodoxy in Germany before the war: Neo-Orthodoxy with its own congregations, and a community-Orthodoxy which resided under one roof with the afore-mentioned liberal and reformist movements.

The diversity reflected in these forms of Jewish life was destroyed by Nazism. The Jewish community in Germany today no longer has anything in common with the prewar community—its religious life began to develop anew as of May 1945. In this context, it should be borne in mind that about 300,000 Jews were living in Germany immediately after the war, 20,000 of whom had survived the Third Reich in hiding or had returned from emigration, and more than 250,000 people, especially from Poland, Czechoslovakia and Russia, who had either been transported to Germany by the Nazis or had fled to the occupied zones in the west to escape the pogroms which took place during the Polish Civil War.

The eastern and central European Jews—in contrast to the few surviving German Jews—adhered to an Orthodox liturgy which had been less influenced by Reform Judaism and liberal thinking. In fact, from 1945 to 1948, there was such a flourish of activity in Jewish religious life in the detention camps, especially in the American occupied zones, that it not only included education and religious services, but even resulted in the printing of a complete edition of the Talmud in Bavaria, for example. But this last blossoming came to an end in 1948, when 90 percent of the "Displaced Persons" left the Western occupied zones in Germany and headed for Israel or North America.

2.

Following a number of conflicts with the tiny contingent of German Jews, the rest of the Jews remaining in Germany chose as their form of religious practice an Orthodox variant of Judaism that was not very stimulating intellectually. It was characterized by a strong orientation to the newly founded State of Israel as well as by a high degree of ritualism.

What role did religion play in this situation? One cannot help but ask to what extent the catastrophe of the Holocaust had an impact on the religious outlook of the survivors. It is true that there were people who had become extremely religious through their experiences; but the overwhelming majority of those who had been religious before the catastrophe were severely shaken in their faith by their experiences in the camps. All this means, however, is that the renewed inclination toward Orthodox religion played a primarily functional role: the contents of the faith now became less significant than the forms in which it was practiced. At this point in history, it was most important to restore a familiar environment, a form of religious ceremony that guaranteed Jewish family life and secured Jewish identity as well as places in which a community could be fostered.

212

In practice, this meant that primarily moderate Orthodox rites were cultivated in the communities of all relatively large West German cities, with the exception of West Berlin; it also meant that, for the most part, Orthodox rabbis were appointed. It should also be noted that the Jewish communities established in West Germany after the war all took the form of *Einheitsgemeinden* (united communities.) These communities were organized as corporate entities under public law, which put them on an equal footing with the churches; as a consequence, they also benefitted from the synagogue taxes collected by the public tax authorities on their behalf. Furthermore, for many years it was generally accepted opinion that, in view of the small number of Jews living in Germany, anything other than a united community simply could not be countenanced.

The situation in East Germany before the Wall came down was somewhat different. The small denominational Jewish community with some 200 members in East Berlin was the only one in existence—aside from the nominal Jewish communities in other East German towns—and it too was predominantly Orthodox in its rites. Corporate entities under public law in the West German sense did not exist in the former East German state.

In postwar West Germany the tasks of the Jewish communities consisted of the following: providing the resources and facilities for synagogal religious services as well as religious instruction, securing the supply of kosher food, maintaining Jewish cemeteries and the corresponding facilities for funerals as well as circumcisions. Up until 1989, all of these tasks were performed almost exclusively according to Orthodox ritual; disregarding the one liberal synagogue in West Berlin and the fact that a liberal rabbi was active in the Mannheim and Hamburg communities, which were officially Orthodox, and later also in Hanover, the predominance of Orthodoxy remained unbroken. In communities such as Frankfurt am Main, liberal religious services were held from time to time (until the

1970s) on a semi-private basis, and they were attended mostly by older German Jews; in other, small communities like Wuppertal, cantors and preachers from North America were occasionally invited to participate in the services.

3.

Nonetheless, given the fact that ever fewer members of the communities knew Hebrew and, in any case, Orthodox Judaism was not being practiced in their day-to-day lives at home, the traditional Orthodox service, the element of piety and the intensity of religious devotion, were obviously in crisis. The traditional core of the Jewish religious service, the reading of the Torah, played less and less of a role; rabbis were only poorly trained to offer halfway interesting and stimulating sermons; each subsequent generation knew less and less about the meaning of the religious services. Moreover, the reactions of the congregations to this decline of consciously experienced piety ultimately came down to an unimaginative repetition of the pat explanation that the community and religious services could hardly compensate for what the family was failing to do at home. Another controversial issue which has played a role in Germany, just as it has in all Jewish communities outside Israel, is how to deal with the non-Jewish marital partners and children of community members. According to the traditional Halakhah, this question is relatively insignificant for women and community members; but more than a few Jewish men who married non-Jewish women have left the community because of it.

The spiritual shortcomings of the traditional and ritualistic Orthodoxy provoked different experiments over the years. In one case, it was the Conservative service offered by the U.S. army which attracted members who no longer wished to take part in the traditional service; in another, it was a rabbi from the Lubavitch movement who held interesting and stimulat-

214

ing services for children and adolescents. Then there were also quite a few Judaeo-Christian circles in which the one or the other was able to fulfill his spiritual needs. Yet the lack of liberal services made itself painfully felt.

The dogma of the united community was not broken until the end of the 1980s. While East German leader Erich Honecker and his government were still in power, the legal heirs of "Adass Yisroel," one of the Neo-Orthodox communities located in East Berlin before the war, were given back the real estate property which had been taken away from the community by the Nazis. After German unification in 1990, with this land as backing, the small Neo-Orthodox community successfully challenged the principle of the united community, and it has earned them the ostracism and hostility of the other Jewish communities. It is noteworthy that the "Adass Yisroel" congregation in the center of Berlin has been particularly devoted to the Russian-Jewish immigrants and is helping these people find a new Jewish identity.

Furthermore, the steady influx of Soviet Jewish immigrants into Germany over the last 10 years has had side-effects which have inevitably left their mark on the religious landscape of the communities. In the short or long run, and certainly by the turn of the millennium, the number of Jews living in Germany will at least double as a result of Russian-Jewish immigration. In fact, the size of this minority contingent alone may even increase to some 100,000 persons. What is of primary importance here is that in Germany, just as in the State of Israel or in the United States, many of these families have non-Jewish members. Moreover, the immigrants know very little about Jews and Judaism due to the generally anti-religious and specifically anti-Semitic policies of the former Soviet Union with respect to Jewish culture and values. The integration of these people into the Jewish communities therefore poses a not inconsiderable problem.

Additionally, a feminist theology which stems from Christianity and which is having a growing impact on public life is beginning to influence Jewish communities—at least those with university-educated female members who support, albeit non-dogmatically, the women's movement. Marginally, at least, a feminist and emancipatory way of thinking is making itself felt.

At long last, and in spite of renewed misgivings over xenophobic incidents, more and more young community members, especially those of the third or fourth generation who have spent most of their lives in Germany, are coming to regard this country as their home. Now they are searching for forms of religious identity that will correspond to their lifestyle.

It is only against this background that one can understand the controversies which have cropped up in several Jewish communities in Germany this year and in the past, and which must seem strange, at least to Americans:

—The comparatively small Jewish community of Heidelberg almost split up over an issue that was related to a new synagogue building: unlike the old structure, it now has a gallery on the second floor, and the women refused to take their places in the gallery during the service.

—The rabbi of the Hanover community, which embraces the liberal liturgy, barely avoided losing his position because he allowed women to touch the Torah as part of the celebration of the Torah (Simchat Torah).

—A Jewish community in the process of being founded, supported mainly by academics in the small university town of Oldenburg in northern Germany, will be adopting a liberal rite.

—The small communities of Brunswick, Wuppertal and Göttingen, revived by an influx of Russian immigrants, will all be adopting a liberal rite.

In other words, Russian immigrants who have entered "mixed marriages," a relative increase in academic Jewish female professionals or women living in academic circles, as well as a desire on the part of young people for an understandable religious service, are developments which are inevitably fueling the desire for liberal services in Germany, which is to say, for some form of religious pluralism in the existing united communities.

Most of the Jewish functionaries in Germany are still convinced that the Jewish communities in Germany can only exist as united communities. This credo is based on the argument that such a small community cannot afford to have different religious denominations existing side by side. This view of things is not correct, at least as far as the purely quantitative side of the argument is concerned. In Switzerland and in the Netherlands, for example, where the Jewish population is no larger than in Germany, Orthodox and liberal communities coexist. So, sooner or later, the nominally Orthodox-oriented communities, especially in Frankfurt and Munich (unlike Berlin), and with them the larger communities in the major Rhineland cities, will have to decide whether they want to offer their members liberal and Conservative services within the framework of the united communities or face the prospect of having groups splinter off. In Hamburg, for example, for some time now a group of community members has been offering a type of religious instruction to families with non-Jewish partners; in Frankfurt, a private association was founded this year for the purpose of establishing liberal services; and in Heidelberg, two liturgies exist side-by-side under very strained circumstances.

At this point, no one can say whether the communities' Establishment, which is intent on defensively safeguarding identity, will be able to satisfy these changed religious demands or whether it will produce the very situation which it sought to prevent in the first place, namely the dissolution of the united community!

One characteristic of the modern age is a more open-minded and religious pluralism. The Jewish community in Germany, while beset by diverse problems and traumata, will also have to face up to this reality sooner or later. As a result of urbanization, higher education and individualization, the religious development in all Western industrialized societies and in almost all of the world's religions generates a critical attitude towards tradition and at the same time more intensive forms of spiritual and ethical religious consciousness and group-building. This is also the case in Germany. Therefore, one can only hope that the responsible authorities will finally see the writing on the wall and fall into step with the dynamics of social trends. It will not help for them to close their eyes to issues and pressing concerns which, for a growing number of Jews, cannot be dealt with effectively by static, ritualized Orthodox practices.

If there has been one thing that has determined the strength of Judaism over the course of more than two and a half thousand years, then it has certainly been that the core of the tradition has always adapted to the circumstances under which the Jews have lived—and it has adapted to them in such a way that this core has not merely been preserved, but actually fortified.

Making a Living—
Jews in German Economic Life

by Igor Reichlin

How do Jews in Germany earn a living nowadays? This question, seemingly innocent, can have an explosive impact. Touch the subject and the conversation stops dead: Why are you digging up the old Nazi ghost? some ask incredulously. After all, wasn't it massive Nazi propaganda about Jewish economic supremacy, their control of the country's shops, factories and banks, that fired up anti-Semitism in prewar Germany and turned law-abiding Germans into assistants to the murder and abuse of the Jews? Why give Jew-haters—that notorious one-seventh of the German population—the slightest chance to buttress their charges with facts?

Such arguments have hindered sociologists from doing the obvious: analyzing the changes in the role the Jews have played in the German economy over the past 60 years.

Close observation shows that even though some Jews nowadays control considerable wealth in Germany, and many live comfortably, a good number are still moving on the fringe of the German economy. Advanced age, fear of the Nazi past, lack of starting capital, latent anti-Semitism and, for many, too recent arrival in Germany are among the causes of such marginalism. But perhaps the key reason is the absence of overlapping social, economic, and cultural networks of the kind that sustained the vibrant life of the Jewish community in Germany before 1933.

Hitler's mad policy mix of racial bias, ultra-chauvinism and destruction of all opposition effectively forced the Jews out of the German economy by almost fully eliminating the Jewish community's economic base and business infrastructure. His policy had enthusiastic support among small- and medium-sized businesses, which understood it as a kind of super-protectionism and seized the chance to profit at the expense of the Jews—their domestic competitors.

With emigration, the Holocaust and disease taking their toll, by mid-1945 the group of Jewish survivors in Germany barely counted 15,000. Between 1945 and 1949, the flood of Displaced Persons boosted their numbers to over 200,000. But for most of these Jews, Germany was only a transit station, a pause between a horrible past and an uncertain future. Rootless, they chose to flee further, to Palestine (later Israel) and the United States, rather than make their home in the war-ravaged but still menacing land.

Fifty years after the war, returning Jews and new immigrants from eastern Europe, Israel and Iran have swelled the Jewish presence in Germany to one-tenth of its pre-Nazi strength, or to around 60,000, but so far they have not been able to rebuild the Jewish community's economic backbone.

The postwar compensation payments to the Nazi victims focused the public debate on how much Germany should pay and to whom rather than on the Jewish economic role iself. So today, while many Jews appear frightened by the very question about their economic activities, non-Jews generally look embarrassed and at a loss for an answer. Many of them are unhappy about continuing payments to the Jews as compensation for Nazi atrocities and are envious of the few publicly known commercially successful Jewish businessmen.

A character in the Rainer Werner Fassbinder★ play *Garbage, The City and Death* describes a Jewish competitor: "He is always a step ahead of you and leaves others nothing but a pittance . . . And he's got banks on his side and the powerful men of this city . . ." While this play was banned for its overt anti-Semitism in the mid-1980s, it was the first attempt by a German intellectual to touch an unspoken taboo. This taboo, like a flying shroud, is still shielding Jewish economic life from the curiosity of outsiders, helping, perhaps, to prevent a revival of envy, which often starts out as ugly and can turn deadly.

To an extent, this taboo has succeeded in blocking out the facts, as is shown by the ignorance the Germans show on the issue. But such ignorance has not prevented prejudice. In recent public opinion polls, 36 percent of Germans say Jews have too much influence in the world and 20 percent say that Jews, who now barely make up 0.01 percent of the German population, have too much influence in Germany. The taboo reflects the contradictions of modern Germany. Although it is a democratic and diverse, pedantic and hard-working country, German society clearly remains very much at odds with itself over the terrible heritage of the Holocaust.

Addressing the issue of Jewish presence in Germany, including the economic role the Jews play here, could help this nation find an easier way out of its moral convolutions. The time has come for this and other taboos to be lifted and replaced with a dialogue.

Yet, what about the fear of neo-Nazis and their virulent anti-Semitism? Could they not indeed misuse facts about the Jewish economic role to support their attacks? Perhaps, but the absence of facts has never stopped a xenophobe from being xenophobic. And surely, half-a-century after the war, German democracy has become strong enough to cope with fringe groups that are trying to pull the country back into chauvinism and intolerance. Germany today can ill afford either because it has become part and parcel of global markets and the international division of labor. These have made the German economy far more dependent on foreign trade than it was when Hitler came to power.

Thus, while in 1932 Germany's foreign trade amounted to 18 percent of its overall gross domestic product, in 1993, foreign trade provided over one-half of the nation's GDP. If only for this reason, it is hardly likely that anti-Semitism will again become a state ideology and a government program.

There are other factors that lead one to believe that Jews in Germany today can now well defend themselves. In 1932, the role Jews played in the German economy was indeed quite prominent, but they were politically divided and had no articulate lobby capable of forcefully expressing their opinion inside and outside the country. The situation at present appears to be the reverse, at least as far as the domestic political lobby is concerned, and its ability to reach public opinion abroad.

Yet, how much economic muscle do Jews in Germany have now? To which income groups do they generally belong? How do they see their future in Germany, the country which their brethren abroad believe Jews should be avoiding? More often than not, the answers to these pertinent questions are vague. This is hardly satisfying; democracy would be more convincing if it had at its disposal hard facts rather than foggy descriptions.

As the country's Jewish community struggles to explain to itself its raison d'être in Germany, and battles against the waking demons of the Nazi past and the burdens of the present, it is worth taking a brief look at what the Jewish community in Germany once was . . .

A Shadow of the Past

Walk on a Friday morning through the quiet streets of Berlin's Schoenhausen area or down Frankfurt's Liebigstrasse, and you are in a ghost town: no housewives popping in and out of a local baker's or butcher's; no tailors, pins between their lips, busily dressing and undressing limp mannequins behind tall shop windows; no delivery carts rattling along cobblestone roads; and no Yiddish babble rising and falling in noisy arpeggios over the tumult and bustle of these once-Jewish quarters. Yet even here, the signs are clear that Hitler's Nazis failed in their attempt to eradicate Jews in Germany: when a woman with a teenaged boy turns the corner, snatches of Russian conversation linger in the air as does the glint of a golden star of David in the low cut of her summer dress. And a Hebrew song drifts out of the window of a cab, whose driver is pulling on his freshly-rolled cigarette, waiting for his next customer.

No, Germany today is not *judenrein*—free of Jews. Jewish communities still count about 42,000 registered members and there are another 10,000 to 20,000 resident Jews who are not registered. It is only when these figures are compared to figures of the prewar years that they pale: in 1933, all Jewish communities combined counted well over half a million members.

The difference between then and now is not just a matter of size. Most Jews who reside in Germany today have little in common with their brethren of 60 years ago, when four out of every five Jewish families had German roots that went back generations; the rest were relative newcomers, whose families had arrived in the first quarter of this century from the eastern provinces of the German Reich. These eastern European Jews were tradition-bound people, whose Orthodox habits, religion and culture set them apart from the increasingly assimilated, Germanized Jews. They were often also poorer, less healthy and less educated than the rest of the German Jewish community and were often among the main recipients of financial aid from Jewish support networks.

Today, only around ten percent of Jewish community members—some 4,000 people—are of German-Jewish descent. A further 15,000–20,000 are families of Displaced Persons who remained in Germany after the war, and East Europeans who immigrated in waves thereafter. About 10,000 Israeli and Iranian Jews joined them in the 1970s, while more than 20,000 Jews from the former Soviet Union have poured into Germany since 1989, bringing the total number of ex-Soviet Jews to about 30,000.

It is clear that the economic role of the recent arrivals is rather limited, for it takes about five years for a settler to fully adapt to the existing economic and social system of the host country and become a net donor to it. Such transformation is already beginning, and small businesses owned by Jews from the former Soviet Union are springing up throughout the country, as the newcomers acquire financial know-how and combine it with whatever capital they have been able to bring out or borrow.

Today's Breadwinners

Sociological surveys of the present-day Jewish community are exceptionally rare. Among the reasons given for such paucity of published information is the already mentioned attitude of government and community officials, who are unwilling to reveal information about the tiny minority for fear it could be abused. The Federal Privacy Act prohibits the disclosure of any data that could harm the people it describes. Thus, it was not possible for the author of this article to obtain lists of Jewish community members in order to conduct a survey of their economic activities, occupations and income levels.

However, there is one study which throws light on our topic: the 1990 publication *Juden in Westdeutschland: Selbstbild und Fremdbild einer Minoritaet* (Jews in West Germany as seen by Themselves and Others) by leading German sociologists Alphons Silbermann and Herbert Sallen. The study, which used a "snowballing method" of polling, shows that 32 percent of Jewish households have a monthly income of between 3,000 and 5,000 Deutschmarks (DM), while a further 40 percent have an income of DM 5,000 or more. For the same period, the data from the Federal Statistics Office show that 26 percent of West German households have an income between DM 3,000 and 5,000 and 12 percent of households have an income over DM 5,000.

Silbermann–Sallen point out, however, that the data for the nation as a whole is not fully compatible with the data on

Jewish households because educational levels and professional structures among employed Jews differ considerably from those among employed non-Jews. While over 23 percent of the Jews in their sample have a high school diploma and over 31 percent have a university degree, among the general population in Germany, these figures are 13 percent and 8 percent respectively. White-collar workers make up almost 70 percent of Jewish breadwinners, versus 52 percent for the general population, but almost 7 percent are blue-collar workers versus over 37 percent for the general population. The self-employed count just over 2 percent of Jews but almost 11 percent of the overall population.

The study also shows that about 46 percent of Jews were fully employed in 1990, which corresponds to the figure for the general population, while about 19 percent were retired versus over 21 percent of the general population. About 30 percent of Jews were over 60 years old, versus almost 21 percent for the general population.

The Destroyed Power

It is interesting to compare these numbers with those gathered 60 years ago. According to the census of June 1933, around 48 percent of Jews were then part of the labor force, about 46 percent were self-employed, over 34 percent were white-collar workers and civil servants, while about 9 percent were blue-collar workers. Close to 16 percent of Jews were over 60 years old and 8 percent were retired. In 1933, Jews, who constituted less than 0.8 percent of the overall German labor force, made up 9.5 percent of all those employed in real-estate, 4.5 percent of those engaged in trading goods and 2 percent of all those active in banking and stock exchanges.

These numbers are even more impressive if the percentages of Jewish managers and owners are considered. In banking and stock exchanges they amounted to 12.7 percent, in industry to 5.5 percent and in real estate to 11.6 percent. (Silbermann-Sallen show that today, about 16 percent of all employed Jews are in white-collar management jobs.) Moreover, in 1933, Jews provided 16 percent of all attorneys, 15 percent of all brokers and commission agents, over 13 percent of all patent lawyers and more than 10 percent of all doctors.

Although already victims of Nazi persecution, Jews still controlled 25 percent of the retail trade, where they had 79 percent of the department store business but only 5 percent of food-store trade; they dominated over 31 percent of the textile industry and 71 percent of the market in ladies' coats. And in 1930, the last year for which such data is available, Jews owned about 19 percent of the banks in Germany, where they provided 7 percent of all top managers and directors. Three years later, although the number of banks had declined, they still held over 50 percent of all banking assets in the country.

Protectionism Ad Absurdum

But time was running out for Jewish entrepreneurs as the Nazis stepped up their Judophobic propaganda and began Aryanizing the German economy by forcing Jews out of business. "When one sees how arrogant these Talmud-thumping Jews are today, it becomes abundantly clear how vital it is to eradicate Jews from the German economy until no traces of them are left. Only then will the German economy blossom fully," claimed one editorial in the *Stormtrooper* weekly by Hitler's chief rabble-rouser Julius Streicher. Spurred on by a combination of hatred towards Bolsheviks and Social Democrats, whom Hitler invariably equalled with the Jews, his racial supremacy theories, which, again, left no room for the Jews in Germany, and, last but not least, by the populist ideology designed to bolster Hitler's support among economic competitors of the Jews, the Aryanization policy of the Nazis represented, perhaps, a unique case of total protectionism conducted by a government. This policy was all the more unusual because it was aimed against an internal economic competitor—Jewish businesses—rather than external competitors—foreign businesses. On the other hand, the Jews were viewed by the Nazis, as well as by many other Germans, as foreigners. Thus, joining in the campaign to "make the German economy German" was for many medium-size German businesses an act of protecting their own market share from a foreign invasion.

As a result of Aryanization, German businesses greatly increased their share of the German market but—and this is important—they did not take over the Jews' foreign business activities. This routinely made German businesses, especially those which expanded through absorbing Jewish companies, far more oriented towards the domestic market. This trend was especially noticeable in banking. Because Jewish banks, with their broad international network of clients and contacts, held more than one-half of Germany's commercial banks' assets in 1933, banishing Jews from the banking industry was paramount to severely hampering relations between the German financial industry and the rest of the financial world.

The long-term effect of Aryanization—as protectionism ad absurdum—became clear much later when the German economy showed signs of lacking the entrepreneurial spirit and international contacts which the Jews had provided it with. Even though the German economy today is highly export-oriented, it is still largely parochial and disinclined to innovate. This is already being recognized in some business circles. Lamenting the absence of innovation and internationalism within German banking, a top German banker points out that in London and New York, many successful investment bankers are Jewish. "We need Jews, too," the German banker says.

A Meek Beginning

Such opinions are a relatively new development because following the defeat of the Nazis, many Germans did not particularly welcome the return of the Jews. A study by the Office of Military Government U.S. in Germany in November 1945 reported that while few people defended the way the Jews had been treated, most felt it had been good to break their economic power. Moreover, the Allied air raids had caused high losses among the civilian population, which many saw as a redress of suffering: victims against victims.

Although there was a certain amount of black-market trading among the Jewish Displaced Persons, very few of the transit community wanted anything to do with rebuilding the German economy. As the Jewish Committee of the American Occupation Zone declared in the late 1940s: "What's to be done? Should we work in German factories? Build German houses? Cultivate German land? No Jew wants to participate in the reconstruction of the economy of a country which destroyed the Jewish people. It would be an absurdity."

Those Jews who had been forced to dispose of their property during Aryanization, often at gunpoint, began a tortuous effort to recover it either by coming to Germany or negotiating through lawyers. For those who had preserved the documents pertaining to the sale, this process was easier, for others it was less so—but for everyone, it was an uphill fight with the German authorities, courts and the new owners.

Meanwhile, anti-Semitism flared up in postwar Germany as vandals desecrated cemeteries and public opinion polls increasingly showed that many Germans felt no responsibility for the damage done by the Nazis to the Jews. Little wonder that very few Jews were prepared to keep the businesses they recovered, and frequently sold them for much less than what they would fetch five or ten years later when the German economy started picking up. Whatever sum was realized through a sale usually left Germany with its owner, although in a few cases, it was invested in real estate in German cities.

Making Up

Yet, once the West German government under Konrad Adenauer decided in the early 1950s that, despite the nation's very tight postwar finances, Germany must begin paying reparations to Israel and compensation to the Jews for the hardship they had suffered at the hands of the Nazis, Jews inside and outside Germany finally received a chance to improve at least somewhat their financial situation. Over the years and up to the present, these payments have amounted to considerable sums. Between 1952 and 1991, the West German government paid out 3.45 billion marks to Israel under the German-Israeli treaty, 67.89 billion marks under the Federal Compensation Law and 3.93 billion marks under the Federal Restitution Law. By the year 2030, the government will have paid out a further 27.1 billion marks under the Compensation Law and 70 million marks under the Restitution Law, mostly to the Jews but also to other Nazi victims. Overall, Germany will have paid out almost 120 billion marks to compensate for the damages of the Nazi regime.

Such major expenditures have never sat well with the Germans, and reparations payments have always been rated negatively in public opinion polls, causing some pollsters to think they have been a key cause in maintaining latent and overt anti-Semitism at a consistent 12–15 percent rate in the population, although the younger the respondents are, the less pronounced such bias is. As Werner Bergmann and Rainer Erb point out in their book *Anti-Semitism in West Germany*, almost 50 percent of Germans in a 1989 survey agreed that many Jews take advantage of the Germans by forcing them to pay for the crimes of the Nazi past, and a further 29 percent said Jews were disliked because they insisted on receiving compensation payments. At the same time, 27 percent admitted being unhappy about Jewish economic power in Germany.

Thus, focusing on Jewish power, real or imagined, has remained an important factor in the German attitude towards the Jews. Even Konrad Adenauer, when asked shortly before his death whether his policy of restitution to Jewish victims of the Nazis and of rapprochement with Israel was based on self-lessness, snorted in reply: "Don't forget how powerful American Jews are!"

A New Chapter

In the early 1980s, the prominent journalist Josef Joffe wrote in an article entitled "50 Years after the Third Reich" that Jews in Germany are not a "normal" sociological sample: "The 'typical' German Jew is likely to live in Berlin, Munich or Frankfurt, he will own a jewelry or jeans store; or if better off, he will make his money in the construction and real estate sector. Yet, even if he is rich, he will not enjoy high socio-economic status simply because he is not part of the German status ladder. He will not be a banker, a judge, a professor, a politician, an editor or a chief executive. He will live in his own, self-imposed ghetto—one out of 6,000 in Berlin, one out of 5,000 in Munich. He will normally not invite Gentiles to his home nor will he circulate in Gentile social settings. For vacations he will choose Israel during Passover or St. Moritz in the winter—probably in search of a spouse for his son or daughter.

"At home, his children will go to German *Gymnasium* (high school) and then to university. Yet, the most important and numerous social contacts of these youngsters will center on other Jews."

Such a melancholy picture is no longer fully true. The influx of Jews from the ex-Soviet Union has drastically changed the profile of the Jewish populace in Germany. New communities are springing up in places where grass already grew high on Jewish cemeteries.

As the new immigrants take root in Germany, their economic initiative might once again inject entrepreneurial spirit into the German economy, bringing with it cross-border connections. Since the war, Germany has followed a generous policy of opening its doors to Jewish immigrants from the ex-Soviet Union. It will have to be even more generous in the future. Such action would provide a convincing argument that Germany has truly changed since Nazi times, undermining claims that Germans remain incorrigibly anti-Semitic. It might help improve understanding between international Jewry and Germans and would provide the German economy with fresh entrepreneurial talent. And it would further enhance an international dimension of the German economy and might bring in more foreign capital.

The continued influx of Jews into Germany would be a crucial development on several counts. If Jews continue to arrive at the current rate, they will help rebuild the Jewish community to about 100,000 by the end of the century. Integration of thousands of newcomers into the German economy and population depends significantly on their economic activity, and on whether they burden taxpayers as permanent recipients of social aid or ease the tax burden by becoming independent entrepreneurs and white-collar workers.

And in a still wider context, their economic integration will serve as a litmus test of the maturity of Germany's democracy and its ability to withstand the pressures of its troubled past and a still uncertain present.

Thanks for the Memories
Reflections on Holocaust Museums

by Hanno Loewy

In the spring of 1993, the opening of a museum received un-precedented publicity in Germany. Never had such an event caused so much argument and controversy.

And this, despite the fact that the museum in question was not in Germany, but in the United States. It is no ordinary museum, however. It takes the idea of a museum to the limits. It is supposed to tell a story about something we can label neither as the present, nor as history. Its objects are not designed to weave a tale about themselves and human creativity, but rather to tell a story about disappearance, the disappearance of human beings. The museum in question is, of course, the Holocaust Museum in Washington, D.C.

The discussion which had already been prompted by the opening of the Museum of Tolerance/Beith Hashoah in Los Angeles in February 1993 became really heated with the in-auguration of the museum in Washington, and soon filled the editorial pages and culture sections of German newspapers and periodicals. And while many of these commentators claimed that there was more of a need for such a museum in Germany than in the United States, this sentiment was seldom accompanied by a willingness to stop and think about what a Holocaust museum actually is.

All at once, the ongoing debate in the United States and in the American Jewish community about these paradoxical centers of a memory that cannot be put to rest was being followed very closely in Germany—and was also being misunderstood, so it seemed, with resolute determination.

According to such German-Jewish critics as Rafael Seligmann and Michael Wolffsohn, it was not just the form of the American memorials, but the very memory of the Holocaust itself which posed a danger—not to Germany's image in the world, however, nor to the hoped-for renaissance of Jewish life in Germany, but a danger to Judaism itself.

Painful debates that had been going on in the United States for 20 years, dating back to the books by Rubinstein, Wiesel and Fackenheim, concerning the significance of the traumatic experience for one's own identity, were suddenly being taken note of in Germany for the first time and introduced into the discussion—albeit it in a highly selective manner.

One of the questions raised, for example, was whether it makes much sense to present the Holocaust on the Mall of the U.S. capital as a foil to America's civic religion, as it were, rather than deal with that country's own history of land appropriation, massacre of the Indians and slavery. Within the German context, this argument then became a ploy for relieving guilt and relativizing the past.

The American debate between people whose personal lives and families had been affected by the Holocaust in ways that were as disparate as their problems with life after the Shoah★ was thus reduced to a normative debate as to whether the Holocaust should be part of identity-formation or not.

In the end, those critics who question whether the memory of the Shoah in Germany would not be better preserved somewhere more removed from politics than a government commission planning a central museum do not even get a word in edgewise. People in Germany are only too happy to delegate responsibility for dealing with the Holocaust to politics, and to Berlin—the new capital city which, with no less than half a dozen memorials and museums, has been entrusted with "taking care of" the Holocaust on behalf of the rest of the nation.

At the same time, the complaint has been voiced that the Holocaust museums in the U.S. have made memory into a plastic world, that their approach to the Shoah smacks of entertainment. This criticism lumps together the two museums in Los Angeles and Washington as if they could be easily compared, whereas they are in fact conceptually completely different. It deliberately ignores the fact that Yad Vashem in Israel also has its souvenir shop, that many a drab concentration camp memorial, be it in Auschwitz or elsewhere, sells dubious postcards and surprises the visitors with re-creations, reconstructions, lovingly arranged still-lifes of terror and models of gas chambers.

In other words, commemoration takes questionable forms, even in the critics' own backyard. How nice that we now have something to get indignant about, and can point a finger—especially if it is a Jewish finger—at American lack of culture.

What we have at the Wiesenthal Center in Los Angeles is a perfect studio production of the Holocaust, right next to Hollywood and Disneyland. It makes no use of originals, but instead takes the visitor on a trip with special lighting effects at a somewhat authoritarian pace and resembles a rather boring ride on a ghost train. At the end, it revives the duly dazed visitor by hitting him with the successful, worldwide activities of the Wiesenthal Center against racism and anti-Semitism and asking for a donation. A self-sufficient system with the one-two punch of scare tactics and tranquillizing injections.

The idea of the Holocaust as merely an extreme case of universal racism, which is the unspoken message you get at the Wiesenthal Center's museum in Los Angeles, meets with considerable favor in Germany. Not only are the real horrors of the Holocaust swallowed up in a mushy interpretation; such "arguments" can also easily be used as a platform for one's own anti-Semitism.

To this day, German society must live with the fact that the social project in which the human beings of this country presumably invested the greatest amount of energy in their history, namely, in annihilating the Jews, quite obviously failed. And now that this society must take responsibility for what happened, it at least wants to say the attempt was not meant "that way."

No German wants to be reminded of the Manichaean struggle between good and evil, of the struggle against the roots of his own civilization. No German wants to be reminded of the nonchalance with which the visionary goal of a civilization "liberated" of its Jewish roots was linked "back then" to the completely banal interests of everyday life in the fierce competition for economic resources and career opportunities. This kind of anti-Semitism in its modern racist guise was not unlike a sports competition: a competition for the most radical solution, a competition for the Führer's love. Anyone who was especially "talented" got ahead, moved up the ladder. Anyone who demonstrated originality called attention to himself, showed that he was fit for the most difficult tasks. No German really wants to be reminded any longer of the frustrated libido, the betrayed ambition, the "global struggle" which ended in "collapse."

As a consequence, all interpretations which supposedly "universalize" the Holocaust, and in fact merely make it seem commonplace to the point of obscurity, are currently *en vogue* in Germany. If one is not allowed to forget the Holocaust—and occasionally even makes a friendly comment about having learned something from the Jewish "culture of remembrance"—then at least it can be continually re-interpreted to the point of irrelevance.

The fact that the Wiesenthal Center is concerned with something entirely different, namely with packaging the Holocaust in such a way that it can actually be used as a substitute for identity and deployed as an instrument of policy, is a completely different matter.

So, whether it is a matter of disciplining American Jews in order to temper any criticism they may have of Israeli politics, or of keeping down-and-out Blacks and Latinos from looting the Jewish store on the corner—when you come right down to it, it is primarily a matter of increasing the influence of the Wiesenthal Center on the Jewish community. For only a "Holocaust" which can happen to you again at any time and any place, which can happen to anyone, a "Holocaust" the harbingers of which are standing on the very next street corner, is no longer personally threatening but instead is a confirmation of your identity. This "Holocaust" is something you can—and must—"fight" against, especially as a Jew (even if it is by sending a check to the Wiesenthal Center), for it is something which helps you to organize and affirm your own life, instead of questioning it. With this kind of thinking, the Jewish history of persecution—this negative headstart with experience, so to speak—leads to a secular, political claim to power.

Yet, strangely enough, the criticism articulated in Germany does not focus so much on the Los Angeles museum and its blatant attempt to make use of the Holocaust to engender Jewish identity. Possibly because such criticism would, if anything, cause the Holocaust to be taken seriously by those who want to put it out of their minds. For all kinds of reasons. Instead, there has been more of a tendency to stigmatize the museum in Washington as a shrine of Jewish identity.

In the German newspapers *Süddeutsche Zeitung* and *Allgemeine Jüdische Wochenzeitung*,* Rafael Seligmann warns against Judaism's "fixation on the Holocaust" and calls for the "time of mourning" to be followed by a "time of rejoicing." Seligmann has had enough of wallowing in a history of suffering, enough of the role of victim and eternal grief, and calls instead for a stand in favor of a "positive Jewish sense of identity."

Yet, the Holocaust has not become the key issue of Jewish identity because it in some way confirms that identity (for example, in the continuity of the role of the victim), but because it fundamentally questions the very core of identity, namely, the possibility of existence itself. The memory of the Holocaust yields a purely negative dimension of identity: an identity shaped by the common experience of existential threat that considered neither assimilation nor Orthodoxy, and spared neither those who wanted to shed their Jewishness, nor those who lived faithfully by the Halakhah. The Holocaust generates at best "a sense of community" only because it represents a common problem for Jewish identity.

How then, after the Shoah, after having experienced the real possibility of complete extinction, can there still be a Jewish identity without an awareness of this sense of threat? The Nazis were not an instrument of God (as some in the ultra-orthodox camp would maintain) sent to test or punish the Jews (for assimilating or otherwise); and by the same token, the survivors were not saved as a result of some divine plan.

The survivors and their descendants basically know very well that their survival, the fact that they continue to live, is just as meaningless as the death of their family members. And it is not easy to take refuge from this knowledge or live with this meaninglessness—regardless of whether we banish the question behind the walls of a museum or try to banish it from our minds with a trick called "positive Jewish identity."

In an article in the German newspaper *Frankfurter Allgemeine Zeitung*, Michael Wolffsohn went one step further than Seligmann. He had looked in the Bible and discovered the commandment against graven images. He had also discovered that in the Washington museum there were photos of the dead, indeed a whole tower full of photos, showing Jewish residents of a Lithuanian community which was almost completely wiped out in a single day.

This is serving graven images—in other words, outright idol worship, concludes Michael Wolffsohn: "Remembering through the word is Jewish tradition. Remembering through the image is a breach of Jewish tradition." Even remembering through stones is un-Jewish, says Wolffsohn, who would then have to include the Wailing Wall. And he goes on to say: "The memorial becomes a substitute for God."

Wolffsohn regrets that Judaism is becoming emptied of religion, laments the fact that "it is no longer religion, but Jewish history, the Jewish situation, that is creating Jewish identity." His conclusion: Holocaust memorials are "profoundly un-Jewish." Which brings the debate down to a level where it becomes pointless.

The museum in Washington was conceived and realized by survivors of the Holocaust and their children, who did not wish to reinvent Judaism but instead to work on their most essential problem—the caesura in the continuity of life, the fissure separating the survivors from the dead, the abyss between those who were lost and those who were saved. The question "What exactly is a Holocaust Museum?" has not been seriously asked in Germany to date. Indeed, it seems as if no one in Germany wants to ask it.

The museums in America merely seem to provide a welcome opportunity for a discussion that has been long in the making—namely, that there can be no German Judaism until the battle between "positive Jewish identity" and "Holocaust fixation" has been decided once and for all.

Yet, what is the core of Jewish identity—and that is a question everyone must ask himself—if not in that duality of origin and religion, which is expressed by the paramount importance attributed to history in Judaism? Surely, Jewish identity resides in the dual determination by (involuntary) origin on the one hand, and the voluntary assumption of the Jewish faith on the other. This forges the inner tension implicit in the concept of the "Jewish people," which is a community based on a common fate and common faith, and which also makes it possible for a non-believing person to be a Jew, and for someone to be a Jew who is not Jewish in origin.

The question as to what story should be told by a Holocaust museum is one that has to be raised in no uncertain terms in Germany as well. Especially since a number of

238

prominent figures in German society today want to add a Holocaust museum to the already considerable collection of memorials in Berlin.

One should indeed ask what the fetishization of objects and their aura in the Washington museum concept is trying to achieve and what needs it is responding to. What is behind the attempt to let these originals speak for themselves, to tell a story which is frighteningly unbelievable, and is at first extremely remote for most museum visitors? It would be appropriate to ask whether this attempt, reminiscent of a relic cult, to "narrate" the Holocaust, may not itself also represent a renewed attempt to respond to the catastrophe by salvaging some sense of meaning.

Then, however, one would not need to be so concerned about the political background of the museum, with the obvious power play between the U.S. government and its interest in having leverage in the Middle East and the interest of the Jewish community in gaining public recognition for its history. Instead, one would have to be willing to recognize in the perfection and helplessness of this museum's "narration" the insatiable yearning of the second generation of Holocaust survivors to have something with which to offset the silence, the trauma of their parents. To find a form of narration which bridges the gap between themselves and their history. One would have to ask about the painful fissure which the Holocaust made in any possible continuity of individual and collective experience; about the need to give oneself a history where only a black hole, a traumatically fractured experience of time, is left. A story whose only meaning seems paradoxically to lie in the camps, is grounded in the story of the Holocaust itself. And often in a devastating, literal sense: The driving force behind the numerous Holocaust institutions in the United States, it seems, is thus a generation of people who have to live with the feeling of having been put on earth to serve as their own compensation for the immeasurable loss, the loss of family members who were destroyed, of a world that was destroyed.

The question which constantly recurs is "why did I of all people survive?"—a question which pursues the survivors and to which there is no answer.

The Holocaust museum does not answer this question either, but there would be little point in having a museum unless it can establish some kind of emotional relationship, if only by issuing a false ID card (of a Holocaust victim) to visitors at the entrance. However, if this museum-bestowed identity is an invitation to the recipient to deny his own history, his own involvement with the society of the perpetrators, this kind of approach is bound to become problematic. Under the old Communist regime in East Germany, the Buchenwald memorial invited its German visitors to identify with the resistance by having them take part in a collective ritual which involved moving through the site itself. The role of the perpetrators, or of the visitors, in the Holocaust was ignored. Young East Germans who came to Buchenwald for official youth ceremonies or induction into the People's Army, for example, had to make their way down to the memorial for dead soldiers and tediously work their way back up the hill to the tower and the plaque with the oath of the prisoners in order to complete their rite of initiation into the anti-fascist movement. On closer examination, a similar mechanism may be at work in the plans to establish a central Holocaust museum in Germany today.

By "universalizing" the fate of the Holocaust victims in such a way that it could have happened to anyone, and then consistently blocking out the perpetrators and their history, people are being invited once again to forget their history and rest at ease now that it has been "commemorated." Even the Allied bombings of German cities can henceforth be dealt with under the heading of "Holocaust" and not by those who continually hark back to the glorious past, but by people who claim to be among the critical progressives in this society. It is then no longer a matter of perpetrators, supporters and collaborators, those countless numbers of people who identified with the perpetrators, either blindly or consciously. It is then no longer a matter of German society as such, but of human beings who were "affected" by it. And in the final analysis, we have all been "affected" by it.

It will become ever more difficult to maintain the irritating effects of memory if this kind of remembering is so good at helping us to forget.

It is hardly surprising that this is happening. For in the collective memory of German society there is in fact no Holocaust. In the biographies of the survivors, the Holocaust is indeed present as a form of exclusion and persecution on a global scale and taken to the point of annihilation in a seemingly consistent and deliberately planned process. However, in the Germans' experience and memory, the Holocaust is at most something which has been put behind them, something in which people were "somehow" involved, but which nobody "really" wanted. That the conflicts within Nazi society, conflicts over influence and resources and, in many cases, competition for the most radical approach, are sometimes interpreted in retrospect as forms of resistance, is only an absurd side-effect of individual and collective attempts to relieve guilt. This must be taken seriously, however, because to many (who lived then and passed on their memories), it was not the motives and interests behind the way people acted in their everyday lives that were determined by anti-Semitism but rather the outlet through which these motives and interests were vented.

This outlet was not simply imposed from above, but rather corresponded to what was often an unspoken agreement. It was based on deeply rooted traditions; it was like an inexorable fight for survival which affected all areas of life and at the same time invited a solution to all problems in one fell swoop. This, of course, makes remembering the Holocaust so difficult for German society, even today.

Hitler is said to have claimed that conscience is a Jewish invention. The projection of inner conflicts by Western civilization onto a counterpart, which is in reality one of its own roots, albeit its most uncomfortable one, this projection of one's own guilty conscience onto "the Jews" was, if you will, at the beginning of the Holocaust. So, realizing that the "Germans will never forgive the Jews for Auschwitz" (Henryk M. Broder) is not particularly original. And for that reason, it is all the more depressing.

Jewish Museums in Germany
A German-Jewish Problem

by Cilly Kugelmann

Jewish museums in Germany do not just present and reconstruct Jewish history and culture; they are simultaneously exhibits of contemporary history in their own right. At around the same time as the past was declared history—marked by a German-American reconciliation ceremony which took place in 1985 over the graves of fallen soldiers and SS officers at the Bitburg★ military cemetery—museums and institutes were set up, in both West and East Germany, with a view to making the history of the Jews in Germany known to a wider audience.

Frankfurt was to be the first German city to have an independent Jewish museum. The museums in other places are departments of municipal or state history museums.

Until only a few years ago the Frankfurt Jewish Community, like all Jewish communities in Germany, was "invisible." Here too, the 1980s was a decade of transition from a community of former refugees to a Jewry whose representatives increasingly began to evoke the tradition of an earlier German Jewry. It was not until the 1980s that the new community center was built, a belated architectural concession to a Jewish future in Germany. Finally, August 1994 saw the consecration of the synagogue in Frankfurt's West End, which has been restored to what it was in 1910. This synagogue, the interior of which was gutted in the *Kristallnacht*,★ was rebuilt in 1953, and services have been held there since. The partial restoration of the interior also docu-

243

ments the recent assimilation of German-Jewish history, which would have been unthinkable only a few years ago.

The Jewish Museum was planned by the Frankfurt city authorities for the late 1980s. Together with its annexes at Börneplatz, the "Judengasse Museum," the permanent exhibition on "Jews in Höchst" in the history museum of Höchst (a suburb of Frankfurt), and the memorial exhibition of what is surely the most famous German-Jewish Reform school in the Philanthropin, the designated purpose of the Jewish Museum was to make visible the prewar topography of the historical, Jewish Frankfurt.

The museum is housed in a building that became famous under the name "Rothschild Palais." It was opened on November 9, 1988, the anniversary of the *Kristallnacht* and thus a date which forged a symbolic link with the history of the Holocaust. The historical background was the destruction of the Jewish museum which existed in Frankfurt before World War II. The Museum of Jewish Antiquities, which was housed on the third floor of the Jewish Community's administration building, was inaugurated on March 6, 1922, and was—so Julius Goldschmidt, one of the initiators, hoped—to ". . . become one of the sights of our city . . ." The exhibits for this museum had been collected by the Society for the Study of Jewish Artistic Monuments, founded in 1897. The collection consisted mainly of ritual objects and documents referring to Jewish holy buildings. However, the museum also staged special exhibitions on historical subjects, such as the history of Frankfurt's Jews, or personalities such as Moses Mendelssohn.

In 1938, only 16 years after it first opened, the museum was liquidated by the Nazis under appalling circumstances.

It is no longer possible to reconstruct exactly what happened to the collection. Apart from a few particularly valuable pieces, which were "saved" as examples of German goldsmithery considered worthy of preservation, a stock of over 1,000 objects was handed over to the municipal loan bank and

244

melted down. On September 15, 1939, the Frankfurt Loan Bank reported to the Reich Minister of Economics in Berlin that 9,920 kilos of melting silver and 5,500 kilos of commercial silver had been received in the form of "deliveries of Jewelry and precious metals from Jews." After the war, within the framework of a restitution program, a commission was appointed whose job it was to trace artworks and books formerly owned by Jews. Of the possessions that had been seized from Frankfurt's Jews, the commission managed to recover 7,867 intact artworks, 1,024 Torah scrolls and hundreds of thousands of books. These objects were distributed by Jewish Cultural Reconstruction to synagogues, Jewish institutions and museums all over the world, but mainly to Israel and the United States. Only 40 Judaica objects which had been on loan from the City of Frankfurt to the Museum of Jewish Antiquities remained in the city. In 1987, these and a number of other objects were handed over to the newly founded Jewish Museum. The date chosen for the official opening was intended as a reminder of the history of the original museum's destruction and of the impossibility of considering post-Holocaust Jewish history without being forever mindful of the mass extermination carried out under the Nazis.

Even in the Frankfurt of the immediate postwar period, there was already evidence of a certain degree of interest in the history of Frankfurt's Jews. When reconstructing the municipal archives, which had been substantially destroyed in an Allied air raid, one of the staff was assigned the task of collecting and reclassifying those documents which referred to the Jewish population. In 1957, the then mayor of Frankfurt, Leiske, suggested that "documents and reports be collected and compiled in a work capable of showing the artistic, intellectual and scientific achievements which were carried out or supported by the Jewish citizens of the early Frankfurt." Memories of the "city of the Rothschilds and the *Frankfurter Zeitung*" were to be revitalized, of Frankfurt's Jewish bourgeoisie, who thus became retrospectively idealized. This project was received with enthusiasm by Frankfurt Jews who had emigrated to the United States, Britain and Israel and who were also eager to salvage a piece of "positive" history from the ruins of the Holocaust. The cooperation between the city authorities and the Jewish emigrants led to the founding, in the early 1960s, of the Commission for the Study of the History of the Jews in Frankfurt, which is still in existence today and has spawned numerous publications. The Commission discussed the possibility of staging exhibitions that would present documents to a wider public. As Frankfurt rebuilt itself after the war, this plan was repeatedly put on the agenda, but was neither implemented nor finally rejected. It was not until the Christian Democrats took over control of Frankfurt's city council from the Social Democrats in 1978 that a decision was made at last. In the spring of 1980, the city council finally voted to found a "Jewish museum," an undertaking which at that time was only of interest to the initiated, as the original conception was strictly academic in its orientation, and took virtually no account of the complex relationship between the Germans and the Jews. The scandal that blew up in 1985 around the performance of a play by Rainer Werner Fassbinder,★ *Die Stadt, der Müll und der Tod* (known in English as *Garbage, the City and Death),* revived awareness of these precarious relations. The debate surrounding the production aroused new public interest in an institution like the Jewish Museum.

Two years later, another conflict led to an unplanned extension to the museum before it had even opened its doors. During excavation work on the site of a new customer service center for municipal utility users, the foundations of a number of houses were unearthed that dated back to the 18th century, when they formed part of the old Jewish ghetto, the *Judengasse* (Jews' Lane). The southern end of the lane, the vaulted cellars on both sides, two ritual baths, the drainage channels and two wells came to light. All at once, in a district that had been redeveloped out of all recognition in the postwar era, a long-forgotten relic of the old Frankfurt reemerged. This time, in contrast to the controversy over the Fassbinder play, it was not the Jewish community at the forefront, but a group of Frankfurt citizens who campaigned for the preservation of the finds. And now the motivation for the protest was no longer, as it had been in the 1950s, a desire to highlight outstanding achievements by individual Jews in art, politics, science and culture, but an interest in history "from below," in the everyday life of ordinary Jews. The *Judengasse* became a symbol for the oppressive and humiliating treatment of the Jews by the Germans, and the area of the city where Jews had been forced to live from medieval times on became synonymous with the ghettos created by the Nazis in eastern Europe. The civic group which campaigned for the preservation of the ruins demanded that building work on the new customer service center should cease and that the excavations should remain as an "open wound" in the city, a "stone witness" testifying for all time against the crimes of the Nazis. Although the analogy between the Judengasse and the Nazi ghetto is not historically accurate, and although the *Judengasse* is surely not an appropriate site at which to leave an architectural-historical "open wound" as a reminder to future generations of the mass extermination of the Jews, this conflict nonetheless indicates that historical debate has taken on a new quality. The argument was over the official practice of remembrance, which was to present history in esthetic, easy-to-swallow doses with a minimum of costs, either moral or financial. The city authorities did eventually decide to integrate the "stone witnesses" into the new customer service center—as a wound that had healed over, so to speak—and to place them under the auspices of the Jewish Museum. The foundations of five houses, two wells and the two *mikvehs* have been rebuilt and stand today as museum exhibits.

This small example shows that Jewish museums in Germany have to contend with a complicated set of interrelated factors. They are at the point of intersection between a kind of reluctant neutrality on the part of the Jewish population and the lofty moral and ideological functions assigned to them by the Germans themselves. The Holocaust is the filter through which German-Jewish history is perceived by both groups, albeit in completely different ways.

In Jewish museum projects, three contradictory and at times mutually inhibiting forces converge. And it is the precarious balance between these forces which forms the basis on which these institutions must define themselves and the contents of their work.

First, we have German society, as represented by the local or national government departments which provide the political and financial backing for such projects. The second factor is the Jewish community, whose history is presented in such a museum. And, finally, we have the museum staff, who reflect the controversies of the two other groups on a professional level.

The latent and overt conflicts which arise from the different interpretations of present-day German affairs in the light of Germany's past influence the work of the museums in a specific way. It is a struggle over the interpretation of the history of the Jews and the universal significance of that history not only for the Germans but also for the Jews themselves.

If one reviews the history of German-Jewish relations since 1945, one can discern five major stages in its development.

1. The immediate postwar period can be characterized in terms of the paradigmatic rejection of any and all relations between Jews and Germans. While a quarter of a million Jewish survivors were waiting in refugee camps to emigrate overseas, Germany was preoccupied with rebuilding its razed cities, integrating refugees from the East and establishing its political allegiance to the Western alliance in response to Cold War pressures. In the face of a "new world order" which now included the German Democratic Republic, the Federal Republic of Germany and the State of Israel, over 20,000 Jews set about establishing new Jewish communities in Germany.

The initial reaction of the international Jewish and Zionist organizations to these Jews was one of radical hostility, thus reinforcing what could be described as a "living-out-of-suitcases" mentality. Plans to emigrate were retained as a utopian perspective for the future, and in the meantime contact with the German population was reduced to the minimum needed for economic survival.

2. In the 1950s and early 1960s, official relationships were established between leading members of the Jewish communities and representatives of German politics over specific issues. The primary function of these contacts was to work out the details of legislation governing reparations and economic aid to the State of Israel, which had not yet been given diplomatic recognition by West Germany. Then, in 1961, after more than ten years of collective repression and denial, during which time even the word "Jew" was a taboo, the crimes committed by the Nazis were brought back into the public eye by what was the German judiciary's first, belated, attempt to deal with the legacy of mass extermination: the Auschwitz trials.

3. One of the first events which began to bring Jews and Germans closer together at a societal level was the student movement of the late 1960s, led by the first generation to be born after the war. Jewish students and other young Jews were able to identify with the German students' protest against the hypocrisy of their parents' generation, which had bought its new economic prosperity by tolerating former Nazis in the courts, universities, schools and in politics. But this consensus based on common socio-political goals was short-lived. The reaction of the New Left to the Six Day War and the resulting criticism of Zionism as well as the condemnation of Israeli government policy gave rise to new tensions and misunderstandings. This condemnation already bore the features of a moral rigor which in the subsequent course of West German history was to become the main criterion for judging "political correctness." The desire for moral impunity, which had

taken shape in an atmosphere of diffuse feelings of guilt, was increasingly manifested in a sense of solidarity with anyone who was identified as a victim of political aggression. "Victims of the victims"—the slogan that was coined for the Palestinians to whom, so the New Left argued, Germany now bore a special responsibility—had the added, exonerating advantage of casting the Nazis' erstwhile victims in the role of present-day aggressors. The Jews had now brought guilt upon themselves for what they were doing to the Palestinians. In the cultural domain, this exoneration principle found expression in films and novels in which directors or writers went back to examine their parents' lives between 1933 and 1945. Not infrequently they came to the conclusion that, under National Socialism, their mothers in particular had been the victims of fateful circumstances beyond their control and were thus deserving of sympathy.

4. It was not until the U.S. mini-series *Holocaust* was broadcast on German television during the mid-1970s that a broader segment of the public became more willing to confront the history of mass extermination. Whereas the student movement was concerned with fascism and National Socialism primarily as political systems, the focus of attention now shifted to the actual experiences of the Holocaust.

In counterpoint to a large number of autobiographical memoirs by survivors, school and university students as well as lay historians produced a flood of local case studies on the policy that had been practiced with regard to Jews in their town or region. As important as this work may have been for those who pursued it, this micro-sociological research into local history was frequently not based on adequate historical criteria. Given the fact that the Holocaust took place outside the boundaries of German towns, compiling eyewitness testimonies and documents on small-town anti-Jewish policies was seldom effective as a method of acquiring a structural understanding either of the impact which the Nazi regime had on the non-Jewish German population or of the process of destruction itself. This research usually resulted in the mounting of commemorative plaques bearing the names of local Jewish citizens who had been driven out or murdered.

It was also during this period, incidentally, that the planning began for most of the Jewish museums and memorials that exist today. In small towns in particular, civic groups pressed for the restoration of former synagogues, many of which had already been sold shortly after World War I by Jewish communities that were in the process of disbanding. Today they are used as municipal arts centers or youth centers. Jews no longer live in these places.

The level of political interaction between Jews and Germans changed as well. Whereas up to that time the Jewish community had been concerned with maintaining a low public profile, conflicts were now carried into the open and took on more radical forms. In 1985, for example, members of the Frankfurt Jewish Community occupied the stage on which Rainer Werner Fassbinder's play *Garbage, the City and Death* was to open, thus preventing the premiere from taking place and eventually forcing the cancellation of the whole production.

5. The latest phase in the recent history of relations between Jews and Germans is unfolding against the background of the collapse of the Soviet Union and the unification of the two Germanies. Positions on National Socialism and the Holocaust are no longer seen by German intellectuals, journalists, artists and politicians as the yardstick for measuring Germany's moral integrity and identity—indeed, they had never been seen as such by the majority of the population anyway. Although there is no connection whatsoever in terms of *Realpolitik* between the Holocaust and the division of Germany in 1945, reunification has been regarded as the definitive end of World War II. But it has become clear—not just since the collapse of Eastern bloc socialism, but ever since Helmut Kohl's well-staged reconciliation with the U.S. at the graves of soldiers and SS officers in Bitburg—that German ef-

forts have been aimed at relegating the Holocaust to history. The theory to justify this approach was supplied in the so-called "historians' debate.★ " While still condemning the Nazi regime and its genocidal policies as an inhuman dictatorship, proponents on one side of the debate suggested that the Holocaust was not an unparalleled or a unique phenomenon, nor was the war against "Bolshevism" entirely without justification. Another sensitive point for Jews is the failure on the part of many to make a distinction between the various groups of victims of World War II and mass extermination. The most recent symbolic ceremony to cement this "all victims together" view of history into a national monument was the inauguration of the "Neue Wache" memorial on November 14, 1993, in Berlin. A pietà sculpture by Käthe Kollwitz is intended to serve as a reminder of the grief—now turned to stone—over the fate of *all* the victims of World War II: the soldiers, the civilian population and the victims of genocide. Not only does this cast a veil of obscurity over the role of those responsible for the murders; the attempt at Christian symbolism here also projects a false image of survival, at least as far as the dead Jews and Romany people are concerned. The mourning mother and widow, crying for her dead son, is a classic metaphor of opposition to conventional war. Yet in the Holocaust, no distinction was made between men, women and children: they were all murdered, and indeed it was the women who had the least chance of surviving the concentration camps.

The ambivalent attitude of many Jews in Germany towards Jewish museums is a reflection of their ambivalent relationship to the country they live in. There are several discernible reasons for these reservations about Jewish museums. For one thing, well over half of the Jews living in Germany come from eastern Europe and are not very interested in German-Jewish history. Almost no large German city, with the possible exception of Berlin, has a population of prewar German Jews who identify with the tradition of their home town. Since

German cultural policy is organized and subsidized by the municipal or state government, the Jewish museums are not privately funded and operated institutions, a fact which, in the eyes of many Jews, makes them "German" institutions. Although there is an appreciable number of affluent Jews in Germany, no institution administered by German authorities can ever expect to receive Jewish financial support. Jewish fund-raising campaigns are mounted exclusively for the benefit of Israeli projects. Very few Jews in Germany are willing to make so much as a small monetary contribution to an exhibition, even if it is devoted to a Jewish subject. This is also true with regard to the funding of facilities operated by Jewish communities, such as Jewish schools or kindergartens. The reason given for this refusal is that, after the Holocaust, it is only right that the German authorities should pay for the institutional life of the Jews in Germany. The small number of collectors who have loaned Judaica to the Jewish Museum in Frankfurt or donated the money for a book or some other object are the exceptions that confirm the rule. Another aspect of this peculiarly negative attitude can be traced to what was a kind of labeling process that has taken place since the war, whereby, in the eyes of the Germans, every single Jew has come to be looked upon as a symbolic representative of the six million Jews who were murdered and the few who survived. In other words, whether they like it or not, Jews are typecast in a role that they consider a gross imposition. According to this role, every Jew is an expert on Jewish religion, the history of National Socialism and the Holocaust; he or she is duty-bound to account for, and accept responsibility for, the policy of every Israeli government. In short, every Jew is a walking conscience. For every social and political conflict, the media—television, radio or press—find a Jew who is expected to state his or her position on the subject. Every political party, every political position has its token Jew whose job is to justify its platform in public and thus morally sanction it. In order to avoid this burden and not be forced into admitting that they simply do not have the knowledge or experience to play the role of an expert, many Jews avoid places where their fate and their history are put on public display or made a subject of discussion. Not surprisingly, contemporaries of the Holocaust are also hounded by similar expectations. Not only are they expected to give an authentic account of their own experiences in the ghetto or the death camps. They are also expected to provide information about the entire machinery of destruction, come up with plausible explanations for it and even take a stand on international policy issues such as the Gulf War, racism, neo-Nazis or ecology.

This brings us to the last of the three factors in our equation, namely, the staff of the Jewish museums in Germany. Although 40,000 Jews live in Germany today—about 10,000 of whom are former citizens of the Soviet Union who have come to Germany during the last five years—hardly any of them are potential staff members for such institutions. One of the reasons for this is that Jews who get a university education in Germany very rarely choose to major in the humanities. Although there is an appreciable number of Jewish lawyers and doctors, there are only very few Jews who have a degree in education, history, sociology, philosophy or teaching. The study of a subject in the humanities requires intensive interaction with the society in which one lives and studies. As I have said, Jews in Germany are willing to do this only up to a certain point. Another reason is that, until 1990, there was no such thing as Jewish Studies in Germany. The academic study of Jewish history, religion and culture is organized according to the model of Christian theology. If historians want to specialize in an area of Jewish history, they must do so autodidactically—there are still no professorships in this field. In other words, it is generally difficult to get academically trained personnel for a Jewish museum. Then there is the additional problem of intellectual and emotional access to the phenomena of Jewish history, which invariably implies a manifest or imaginary process of morally and emotionally coming to terms with the Holocaust. This process can take completely different forms, depending on whether the potential museum-worker is Jewish or not. The confusion of identity which shaped the adolescence of today's Jewish adults who grew up in Germany during the postwar period necessarily also has a powerful impact on their interpretation of Jewish history. Often enough, they are strongly influenced by the survival experiences of their parents, who tend to turn these experiences into the only valid philosophy on life. The Zionist interpretation of Jewish history plays a prominent role here, as becomes especially clear in the planning of exhibitions on the theme of mass extermination, or larger overall presentations. Questions such as those related to the assessment of Jewish resistance to the Nazis or how the Jewish councils perceived their role in the ghettos can trigger far-reaching controversies and conflicts. The issue as to how much or how little emphasis should be placed on the Holocaust in a permanent exhibition, i.e., to what extent it is suitable as an instrument for the retrospective interpretation of all of Jewish history, is also hotly debated. The reception given to what was surely the largest exhibition on Jewish culture ever staged in Germany is a good example of this. The organizers of "Jewish Worlds," which was shown at the Gropius building in Berlin in 1992, were accused of having paid too little attention to the history of suffering under persecution. Consequently, the wish (usually voiced by Jews) to have the history of the Jews presented in an affirmative, positive light has been at odds of late with the call (mainly from Germans) for more attention to be devoted to the traumatic aspects of this history.

German staff members have comparable mental blocks of their own, especially if their commitment to the task of educating people about anti-Semitism is based on their opinions and feelings alone, without much knowledge of the precise details. For example, a desire to combat the anti-Semitic prejudice that most Jews were and are rich may prompt some to suggest that exhibitions should focus mainly on poor and lower middle-class Jews. Personal preconceptions also in-fluence the more fundamental issue of whether a Jewish mu-seum should present Jewish history from a Jewish standpoint, based on Jewish sources, or whether instead it should provide a picture of the overall social context.

To conclude this brief outline of the many problems related to the work of a Jewish museum in Germany, it should be added that the period since 1945 has been one of constant and radical change which, for a long time to come, will prevent us from acquiring the kind of critical distance that may be necessary in order to approach Jewish topics. This may be less of a problem in the world of literature, which is a pluralistic context that can tolerate many different texts coexisting side by side. By contrast, exhibitions or indeed museums, not to mention memorials at historical sites, document for a longer or shorter period of time the *whole* context of meaning that has been defined for them and thus monopolize the historical memory inherent therein. We need to realize this in order to remind ourselves of the fact that every project which a Jewish museum in Germany undertakes today is still tied into a period of conflict-based consensus-formation. No exhibition and no museum can ask for more than to be the expression of a conflict of interpretation which is still very much a living issue in the context of postwar history.

The Future of the Past—
Jewish Archives in Germany

by Peter Honigmann

The Jewish community in Germany today is small and insignificant. Until recently, the written material documenting a
magnificent history was regularly taken out of the country
and preserved abroad for historical research. This modus op-
erandi was considered sufficient. Why is it, then, that Jewish
archives are gradually being set up in Germany once again,
and why are efforts now being made to get hold of and work
with documents dating from both the postwar period as well
as previous eras? Put another way, why is it that 40 years had
to pass after the end of the war before any serious attempt was
made in Germany to collect material on Judaism and the
Jews? And if it can be done now, why was it not possible before?

Four factors seem to have contributed to this circumstance,
namely, the length of time that Jews have been present in
postwar Germany, the interest German historians have shown
in Jewish topics, the fact that there is now a new generation of
German Jews in exile, and the end of Communism in eastern
Europe. Maintaining a proper archive system has something
to do with being firmly rooted. As long as Jews are considering emigrating, as long as immigrants are so poorly integrated
that they barely have a command of the local language, there
is no pressing need for archives. In such situations, a function-
ing social system, for example, tends to take priority. It did
not become clear until the 1980s that the Jews in Germany
were here to stay.

It also took decades for academic historians in Germany to develop an interest in the fate of the Jews and to create the corresponding facilities and organizational framework for research. The Gesellschaft zur Erforschung der Geschichte der Juden (the Society for Research on the History of the Jews) was first established in 1988; academic publications such as *Menora* and *Aschkenas* did not appear on the scene until the early 1990s. Thus, at long last, the prerequisites for the preservation and utilization of source material on Jewish history were in place, on both the Jewish and the non-Jewish side. Independently, conditions outside Germany began to change as well. In order to understand how all of these various aspects are interrelated, we need to delve back into history.

The Gesamtarchiv der deutschen Juden (General Archive of the German Jews) was set up in Berlin as early as 1905. This institution was supported at the time by two large Jewish organizations, the Deutsch-Israelitischer Gemeindebund (German-Israelite Community Federation) and the German chapter of the B'nai B'rith order. From the time of its inception until 1939, the General Archive collected more than 200 shelved meters of archive material from Jewish communities, organizations and individuals throughout the Reich. These files were subsequently confiscated by the Reichssippenamt (Reich Office of Genealogy), but most of them survived the Nazi period and the war. In the early 1950s, a sizeable share of this material was transferred to the Central Archives for the History of the Jewish People in Israel. The rest was confiscated by the East German regime and researchers were barred from using it. It was not until Erich Honecker reversed the official policy on Jews a few years before the collapse of his regime, that the "Centrum Judaicum" was established in East Berlin and Honecker agreed to make this valuable collection of archive material from the prewar period accessible for use. Thus, half a century after they had been removed, the documents were supposed to be returned to the premises in which they had been housed before the war. After German unification, the City of Berlin assumed the costs of the "Centrum Judaicum," and the Jewish Community was given a voice in the center's affairs.

However, the exile of the documents on German-Jewish history is not yet over. The bulk of the material is still being stored outside Germany and will also remain there. In the wake of the *Kristallnacht*,★ the Nazis proceeded to confiscate all Jewish documents. The General Archive's collection consisted essentially of donated material and thus comprised only a portion of all the documentation which actually existed. Most of this material was still held by the communities and organizations at the time; and this was now appropriated by force. The confiscated material which was found on West German territory after the war was transferred to the Central Archives for the History of the Jewish People in Jerusalem. An exception was made only in the case of the Hamburg files, which had been deposited in the Hamburg Public Archives by the Jewish Community itself in 1938–39. The documents from Breslau (today known as Wroclaw) were not sent to Jerusalem either; they are preserved in the Jewish Historical Institute in Warsaw. Otherwise, most of the community documentation which has survived is currently in Israel. Only ten years ago, the smaller stocks of material which occasionally came to light were still being sent to Israel. Such a policy was entirely justified in the immediate postwar period. However, now that the history of the Jews has become an established field of research in Germany, and since it has turned out to be extremely difficult to make use of documentary resource materials stored in Israel, there is less of an inclination to export material. After reunification, when records from the prewar communities were discovered on the territory of former East Germany, no one seriously considered sending them to Israel.

After the collapse of Communism, other documents on German-Jewish history moved into the research limelight. It was not until 1990 that the public became aware of some 3,000 shelved meters of German files which had fallen into the hands of the Red Army during their advance and which were stored in a special archive in Moscow. This trove included extensive material of Jewish provenance, which had previously been confiscated by the Reichssicherheitshauptamt (Reich Central Security Office). It contains, for example, the collection of materials from the archive of the Centralverein deutscher Staatsbürger jüdischen Glaubens (Central Association of German Citizens of Jewish Faith), which was one of the large prewar organizations of German Jewry. Moreover, the material in Moscow also includes records relating to various Jewish communities and individuals. There is a clear willingness on the part of both Russians and Germans to return the Jewish material to their rightful owners, but no one quite knows to whom. The original owners no longer exist. And whenever an attempt is made to find successors, then several institutions immediately come forward with their claims.

The archives of the Leo Baeck Institute in New York, for example, have expressed an interest in having the material. This institute was founded in 1955 by Jewish emigrants from Germany, and maintains research facilities in Jerusalem, London and New York. It was founded with the goal of compiling a collection of material that would be as complete as possible in order to provide the basis for in-depth research that would ultimately offer a comprehensive picture of German-Jewish history. Since most of the community documents had already been transferred from Germany to Israel, the Leo Baeck Institute concentrated its efforts on collecting records and documentation from the estates of German Jews who had emigrated. However, the degree of interest in the history of their ancestors' community has already declined sharply among the second generation of emigrés. When the Leo Baeck Institute has completed the comprehensive picture of German-Jewish history it is assembling, then it will have achieved its goal. In the long run, it will not be possible for the legacy of German Jewry to be administered in exile. This, too, is one of the bitter consequences of being driven out.

Although it looked as if Jewish-origin source materials would follow the survivors and leave Germany after the war, this process has meanwhile come to a halt. German historians have become reliable partners in research on Jewish history. And the Jewish community itself is no longer sitting on packed suitcases. Germany has again achieved a certain degree of credibility as a location for Jewish documents. The outcome of the negotiations for the return of the files in the Moscow archive will show just how much trust it can be given.

For the most part, the Jewish archives in West Germany were not set up according to any preconceived plan or design. In 1959, the idea of setting up an archive for the Central Council of Jews in Germany was first mooted. The failure of this initiative is all the more regrettable since, at the time, the highly experienced Jewish archivist Bernhard Brilling was available to tackle the job. Brilling had worked at the Silesian-Jewish Provincial Archive in Breslau before the war and could have guaranteed a certain amount of continuity. The Central Council also passed up another valuable opportunity. Had a central Jewish archive been established at a relatively early date, it might have been possible to avoid the extensive fragmentation which plagues efforts to archive Jewish resource materials today. In the event, there was no coordination to the founding of local institutions concerned with compiling and documenting materials on Jewish subjects. The Central Council's own archive facility was not established until 1987. The Central Archive for Research on the History of the Jews in Germany was set up with support from the federal government. It is based in Heidelberg because that is where the College of Jewish Studies, also operated under the auspices of the Central Council, is located. The archive is completely dependent on public funds. However, as an institution of the Central Council, it can claim to be the successor to the General Archive. This claim is not just based on the fact that it is administered by a Jewish umbrella organization, but also on the idea of centralization. Given that not even large communities are in a position to set up or maintain their own archives, a central archive service is being established for all of the Jewish communities and organizations.

A centralist conception along these lines already met with resistance at the turn of the century. All of the large communities kept most of their records in their own possession. Only the Berlin Community transferred its holdings to the General Archive, which was in the same place, in Berlin. But with the exception of Breslau, where the Silesian-Jewish Provincial Archive came into being in 1924, the wish for regional Jewish autonomy in archive matters remained unfulfilled. Relatively strong, state-supported research and documentation centers with an interest in local Jewish history were not set up until after the war, under completely different circumstances. The Institut für die Geschichte der deutschen Juden (Institute for the History of German Jews) was opened in Hamburg in 1966. Although the latter is a full-fledged research institute, the reason for founding it—and the principal basis for the research conducted there—were the reams of prewar documents from the local Jewish Communities of Altona, Hamburg and Wandsbek, all of which had been preserved in the Hamburg State Archive. The Salomon Ludwig Steinheim Institute, founded in Duisburg by Julius H. Schoeps in 1986, is also a research facility. It has built up an important photo archive by acquiring the estates of various photographers. The Frankfurt Jewish Museum, opened in 1988, also has its own archive department. These relatively well-endowed institutions have only one disadvantage: they are not administered by Jewish organizations. Before the war, the government and the German public left it largely up to the Jews to archive their historically valuable documents; today, although there is a noticeable public interest in such activity, reservations on the part of the Jews tend to stand in the way of a closer working relationship. These reservations are not felt so much in the case of documents from the prewar period, but rather in the case of new, postwar material. As far as people and cultural background are concerned, the Jewish communities in Germany today are not the successors of the prewar communities which were wiped out by the Nazis. Thus, there is relatively little interest in administering historical archive material that was removed from its original location long ago and then became someone else's property for decades. However, when it comes to handing over self-generated written material, and a lot of this has accumulated over the past 50 years, the Jews are not so generous. Generally speaking, the Central Archive in Heidelberg is the only trustworthy partner to which the Jewish communities and organizations will consider releasing material; and even then, the documents do not change ownership. This is another working principle which Heidelberg has adopted from the previous General Archive: documents on loan remain the property of the lending institution, which has the final say as to how they are used and who may use them.

The aspect of access and utilization has always been one of the main arguments in favor of leaving material at the location or in the region where it was generated. It is well-recognized that the greatest interest in a scholarly appraisal comes from the endeavor to write local history. This argument was cited by the Society for the History of the Israelites in Alsace-Lorraine already at the turn of the century when it refused to turn over the materials it had collected to the General Archive in Berlin. And such considerations still play a role today. However, modern communications technology has made it much easier to make use of archive materials from a distance. Documents can be copied and faxed without difficulty. Detailed indexes, with special computer systems now available to compile them, have become the most important bridge between the central archive and interested parties at the site where they originated.

The Central Archive in Heidelberg was founded at a time when the very idea of assuming responsibility for documents from the prewar period was almost unthinkable. The material that had been discovered on West German territory had long since been sent to Israel. What was left of the General Archive was locked up in then still existing East Germany. No one knew about the German-Jewish archive material in Moscow at the time. As a result, efforts initially concentrated on acquiring more recent written material which had originated among Jewish communities, organizations or individuals after 1945. This concentration made particular sense since very little interest was shown by parties outside Germany in acquiring more recent documents, as opposed to prewar material. This remains the case to this day. The time and effort it takes to process modern material far outweigh the benefits of having such material for an archive in, say, Jerusalem or New York. These days, even small communities generate enormous amounts of paper. An initial inventory of stock, for example, showed that around 400 meters of shelved material had already accumulated in Hamburg since 1945. The situation is not much different elsewhere. It took two trucks to transport approximately 300 shelved meters of files from Frankfurt to Heidelberg. Even after piles of receipts, invoices, bank statements, ballots, and the like have been jettisoned in first rounds of sorting, there is still a huge quantity of paper that needs to be stored and preserved.

These documents are not only put in an archive for the purpose of historical evaluation; they are also consulted with remarkable frequency for official purposes by the donating body. There are heirs to be identified and located, property rights to be documented or Jewish descent to be proved in the case of marriage or emigration to Israel. There are also repeated requests for files on the immediate postwar period to justify pension claims. None of this kind of information has any value for world history, but it is of some value to those directly affected. This actually makes it easier to acquire material for the archives. Fifty years after their rebirth, the communities in Germany find themselves swamped by such large quantities of documentation that they do not know where to put it all or how to keep tabs on it, but still need access to it from time to time for verification purposes. This more or less technical circumstance is another reason why Jewish archives have begun to spring up in Germany again 50 years after the war. Up to now, there has been enough cellar and attic space to store documents no longer needed in day-to-day business. The volume of documentation has increased more or less at the same pace as the appreciation of its historical value. It was not until the 1980s that it really became clear that there would be a permanent Jewish community in Germany again. And this realization has gone hand in hand with a growth in interest among the members of the community in their own history. And precisely because this German-Jewish postwar history is less interesting for the Jewish world as a whole, there is a future for its documentation in Germany.

The *Speaking Out* Who's Who

Peter Ambros was born in 1948 in Czechoslovakia. A writer, historian and translator who has lived at various times in Trnava (Czechoslovakia), Jerusalem and Toronto, he is now resident in Berlin, where he writes for the German media and for cultural publications in Prague and Bratislava. He is currently working on his own novel, *The Last Concert*.

Wolf Biermann was born in 1936 in Hamburg. At 16, he moved to East Berlin where he soon made a name as a poet and singer. He became an outspoken opponent of the East German regime; in 1965, he was barred from holding any kind of job and forbidden to appear on stage. In 1976, while he was on a concert tour in West Germany, he was declared a persona non grata and stripped of his citizenship in his absence. He has continued to write and sing, and has received numerous prizes. He recently translated from Yiddish into German a poem by Auschwitz victim Jizchak Katzenelson on the dying of the Jews in the Holocaust. Wolf Biermann lives in Hamburg.

Henryk M. Broder was born in 1946 in Katowice, Poland. He moved to Germany in 1958, went to school in Cologne and currently lives in Berlin. He is a prolific writer of newspaper and magazine articles and has a number of books to his credit, including *Have Mercy on the Germans* and *A Fine State of Affairs: Traveling through the New Germany*.

Micha Brumlik was born in 1947 in Switzerland. Professor of education at the University of Heidelberg, he lives in

Frankfurt, where he represents the Green Party on the City Council. He is chairman of the steering committee of the Jewish-Christian group of the German Evangelical Church Congress. Micha Brumlik publishes extensively on topics related to the philosophy of education and religion. He is co-editor of the intellectual Jewish periodical *Babylon*.

Ignatz Bubis was born in 1927 in Breslau, Germany (now Wroclaw, Poland). A successful entrepreneur in Frankfurt, he is the chairman of the directorate of the Central Council of Jews in Germany and an executive member of the Free Democratic Party.

Ernst Cramer was born in 1913 in Augsburg. He is a journalist and was instrumental in putting the German press back on its feet in the decades after the war. Today, he is senior editor and deputy chairman of the board of trustees of the Axel Springer publishing house in Berlin.

Ralph Giordano was born in 1923 in Hamburg. He first worked as a journalist, later as a documentary film-maker for German television stations. His outstanding work has earned him numerous prestigious prizes and an honorary doctorate. He is the author of many books, both fiction and non-fiction, including his family saga *The Bertinis*, works which reflect his worldwide experience as a television man, and commentaries on the Germans.

Elvira Grözinger was born in 1947 in Poland. She moved to Israel in 1957 and to Germany ten years later. She is a translator and teacher; an active member of the Jewish community, she has been personal assistant to Ignatz Bubis and she is now teaching Yiddish at the University of Potsdam and working as an academic researcher at the Moses Mendelssohn Institute.

Yael Grözinger was born in 1973 in Frankfurt. She is studying medicine at the University of Frankfurt.

Peter Honigmann was born in 1952 in East Berlin. After his studies in physics, he worked at the Academy of Sciences of the German Democratic Republic. In 1984, he moved to

France, where he took up Talmudic studies at the yeshiva in Strasbourg. Since 1991 he has been the director of the Heidelberg-situated Central Archive for Research on the History of the Jews in Germany.

Uri R. Kaufmann was born in 1957 in Switzerland. He studied at the Hebrew University in Jerusalem; he is currently an academic researcher at the Center of Jewish Studies in Heidelberg. The author of a number of publications on Jewish topics, he is the editor of *Jewish Life in Germany Today* (1994), a book available in English from Inter Nationes, Bonn.

Cilly Kugelmann was born in 1947 in Frankfurt. She studied in Jerusalem and Frankfurt; since 1988, she has been working at the Jewish Museum in Frankfurt. She is a co-editor of the intellectual Jewish magazine *Babylon* and author of numerous articles.

Hanno Loewy was born in 1961 in Frankfurt and studied at the University of Frankfurt. He has worked as an exhibition curator and journalist; he is currently director of the Fritz Bauer Institute, a study and documentation center on the Holocaust. His publications include *Holocaust: Limits of Understanding* (1992).

Sofia Mill was born in 1949 in Leningrad, where she received an advanced engineering degree in paper chemistry. She moved to Germany with her family as a quota-refugee in 1992, and she is still looking for work.

Jalda Rebling was born in 1951 in Amsterdam, and grew up in the German Democratic Republic. In the tradition of her parents, she became a singer of Yiddish songs and joined the family ensemble in 1979. She is one of the initiators and organizers of the Berlin Yiddish Culture Festival, held annually since 1987.

Igor Reichlin was born in 1949 in Kazakhstan. He moved from the Soviet Union to the United States in 1981, and from there to Germany in 1987. He studied in both Leningrad and New York; today he is an American journalist living in

Frankfurt and running the German branch of an international financial news agency.

Richard C. Schneider was born in 1957 in Munich. He spent ten years working in the theater in various European cities as a dramatic advisor and director; since 1986 he has been active as an author and journalist for newspapers, magazines, radio and television. His book *Between Worlds—A Jewish Life in Contemporary Germany* appeared in 1994.

Julius H. Schoeps was born in 1942 in Sweden. He is professor of German-Jewish history at the University of Potsdam, and director of the Moses Mendelssohn Center for European-Jewish Studies. In 1993, he was appointed director of the Jewish Museum in Vienna. He is the author and editor of numerous publications.

Rafael Seligmann was born in 1947 in Israel and moved to Germany ten years later. He studied in both Tel Aviv and Munich, where he now lives and works as a writer. He was the founder and editor-in-chief of the Jewish newspaper *Jüdische Zeitung*; he is the author of the German-Jewish contemporary novels *Rubinstein's Auction* and *The Yiddishe Mamme*. His articles appear regularly in the German media.

Susan Stern was born in 1944 in England. Educated in the United States, she has been living in Frankfurt since 1971. A university lecturer, writer and journalist, she is the author and editor of a number of books on Germany, including *Meet United Germany*, *Ten Went West* and *These Strange German Ways—The New Book*. She is involved in the German/American-Jewish dialogue.

Todd Weinstein was born in 1951 in Detroit, Michigan, but has made New York into his city. Photographer, gallery owner and publisher, he is happiest when he is prowling the streets with his camera. His photographs have been exhibited in galleries and museums throughout the United States and are in public and private collections throughout the world. He is currently planning an exhibition on images of Jews in Germany.

Michael Wolffsohn was born in 1947 in Tel Aviv and has been living in Germany since 1954, although he chose to do his military service in Israel. He is professor of modern history at the University of the German Armed Forces in Munich, the author of numerous scholarly articles and almost 20 books, including *Israel: Polity; Society; Economy* and *Eternal Guilt? Forty Years of German-Jewish-Israeli Relations*, both published in English in the United States.